canvas
flying,
seagulls
crying

By the same author

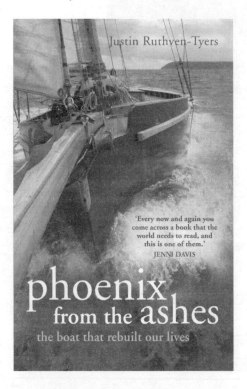

Phoenix from the Ashes: The Boat that Rebuilt Our Lives
ISBN 978-1-4081-5141-9

'Touching... hilarious... a great example of what can be
achieved with a little ambition and a lot of hard work.'
(*Telegraph*)

'The book is a true inspiration.' (*Offshore*)

JUSTIN TYERS

canvas
flying,
seagulls
crying

FROM SCOTTISH LOCHS TO CELTIC SHORES

ADLARD COLES NAUTICAL

BLOOMSBURY

LONDON · NEW DELHI · NEW YORK · SYDNEY

Published by Adlard Coles Nautical
an imprint of Bloomsbury Publishing Plc
50 Bedford Square, London WC1B 3DP
www.adlardcoles.com

Bloomsbury is a trademark of Bloomsbury Publishing Plc

First edition published 2014

ISBN 978-1-4729-0980-0
ePub 978-1-4729-1260-2
ePDF 978-1-4729-1261-9

A CIP catalogue record for this book is available from the British Library.

This book is produced using paper that is made from wood grown in
managed, sustainable forests. It is natural, renewable and recyclable.
The logging and manufacturing processes conform to the environmental
regulations of the country of origin.

Typeset in 10 pt Sabon by MPS Limited
Printed and bound in Great Britain by CPI Group (UK) Ltd,
Croydon CR0 4YY

Note: while all reasonable care has been taken in the publication of this
book, the publisher takes no responsibility for the use of the methods or
products described in the book.

This book is dedicated to the people of Islay: islanders, in-comers, visitors

All illustrations are by the author. These and further examples of his work can be ordered at www.justintyers.co.uk

Justin likes to hear from readers – particularly where on the planet they are, how they heard of the book, and what they did and didn't get out of it. Please get in touch at: justin@justintyers.plus.com

Written with the support of Creative Scotland

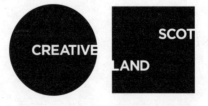

CONTENTS

NOT TO BE USED FOR NAVIGATION

1 BOAT CRASH SPECTATORS

EVERYONE YOU MEET IN THE WILDERNESS is going to be odd – you just have to accept that. What would any 'normal' person be doing out here?

We'd arrived by boat – our boat, which is also our home. Even experienced mariners would find the rocks which guard the entrance to Inner Loch Tarbert on the Scottish island of Jura discouraging. Linda and I only narrowly avoided wrecking ourselves.

Most of the rocks are hidden just below the surface, scattered about at the point where the loch is narrowest, so if you wish to pass through to the quiet waters beyond you have to run their gauntlet, there's no 'giving them a wide berth'. And just to add spice to the tricky navigation the loch is like a river that runs fast in both directions – six hours in, six hours out.

As we approached we found ourselves carried in by a tidal stream which was if anything *too* obliging. It was literally falling over itself to help us on our way. And not only that but explosions of wind were being prepared for us high in the mountains to our right, and hurled down at us whenever it looked as though we might be losing speed. The Almanac warned us that these explosions were a local phenomenon whenever the wind was strong, and in the south. It gets corralled by an unseen hand high up in the mountains and when too much has been gathered together, a gate is broken and the whole lot stampedes downhill to arrive across the decks of boaters at a full gallop.

Our own boat is a self-built version of those lovely old coastal craft you sea in oil paintings from the 1800s; she carries over a 1,100ft of canvas (100 sq m) and although she enjoys a bit of wind as much as the next boat, too much of it sends her into a frenzy. Invariably, when one of those parcels of wind was hurled down at us we'd be at a tricky bit, lost, nervously scanning the chart and looking around in vain to confirm our position. We wanted to stop, pause for breath, take stock of things, and establish where exactly amongst the litter of chart symbols we were – but what with the tide under us, and the wind screaming through the rigging, we were driven on through the kelpie rocks at a helluva pace; forcing the tiller this way and then that, following a hunch... then changing our minds when a head of rock slowly emerged in front of us.

Linda screamed – it's her way of letting me know that she's not happy. A moment later her scream echoed back to us. Startled, we turned to see who else was in trouble.

Because the rocks are unmarked, on the hills surrounding them – half-buried in fern which grows to head-height – islanders maintain three 'transits' as an aid to navigation. Every couple of years they drive across the wilderness on quads carrying tins of white paint to refresh pairs of stones – fortuitously placed by nature – which, viewed in line, guide mariners along a zigzag course through the rocks below. It's difficult to pick these painted stones out at first amid the grand scenery which rolls into the distance all around. Sometimes they will be on the hill ahead of you, and sometimes the one behind – meaning you have to turn and face backwards whilst guiding your ship ahead *and* you'll have to monitor two pairs at once – one lot so that you don't wander from the course you're actually on, and the second lot to see when *they* come into line. Because when they do, it's time to turn. *Now.* Without a moment to lose.

Suddenly the loch opened out and the water became placid. That we emerged the other side of those dangers was mere luck; we pressed on and, following our progress with a finger on the chart, felt our way in to the upper reaches of the Loch. The further in we went the more the wind was tamed by the twists and turns we took around nooks and crannies of land.

We slipped through a naturally-formed canal which was so narrow you could have stepped off the deck and onto a rocky shelf on either side. A goat with his back to us grazing on herbs growing from cracks in the rocks thought he heard something. He lifted his head, throwing a fine set of horns into the air, then stood operating his lower jaw. Suddenly he noticed a gaff-rigged yacht behind him. His hooves slid as he galloped on the spot on hard rock. Then they found some traction, and he bolted for cover into a thicket of silver birch. We turned too late on the next corner, touched a 'table' rock on the sea bed, and heard the metal shoe which protects our long keel scrape as we slid off it again, harmlessly.

There was some confusion over which side to pass a mid-stream rock right ahead of us then moments later we drifted into a pool which was worth ten-times the drama of reaching it. Down went our anchor into clear water like brown glass. The clanking of our chain came back to us from the hills which surrounded us. After that it was so quiet we could hear the chain drip.

We unbent ourselves from our adventure and stood without speaking to see what we'd come to. Language is not powerful enough to describe the silence. It's one thing to stand in an empty and quiet room, but to be able to see hills rising and falling one behind the other, losing themselves in the vague distance of miles, and yet still hear nothing is baffling – you quite literally can't believe your ears. We whispered.

'Will we be all right here?'

'Yes... perfect.'

We'd been living on board for four years. We could scarcely believe it ourselves. Four years idly drifting along the Celtic shores of Scotland, Ireland, France and Cornwall; nosing about in historic fishing harbours, or quietly carrying out our daily chores in deserted anchorages; wandering ashore to meet the quirky characters who inhabit the windy seafronts, getting on nodding terms with the shadowy figures who lurked at the pier-head, and sometimes falling into the open arms of

Celtic Cross

self-appointed ambassadors for the area who wanted us to know what an honour we were doing them simply by bringing our rakish-looking craft into their harbour.

Living on board, summer and winter, browsing the low water shore, felling wood for our fire, and planning our next journey, we felt as though we'd pulled into some lay-by in life whilst the helter-skelter madness of the world passed by. Our contented days were filled – over-filled, really – with purpose and the busyness of self sufficiency.

We were coming to the end of a thrilling summer during which we'd spent our time around the Hebrides, veering off the well-beaten sailing-tracks to try and gain some of the *local knowledge* which Almanacs are always banging on about and insisting you have before you set-out. For us the only way to gain experience of a thing is to throw ourselves in at the deep end and see if we can touch the bottom, so to speak. Taking that as our religion we'd stuck our bowsprit into the outrageously pretty spots along Scotland's Wild West coast discovering places the locals were trying to hush-up and keep for themselves by giving them frightening names like *Witches Cauldron, Grey Dogs,* or *The Sea of Disappointment.* We intruded into these treasures, found that we were welcome after all, and lived little chunks of our lives there in quiet contentment amid the unspoilt panoramas. A day lost in wonder is a day well spent.

Some of our nosing about was simply reconnaissance – spying out likely sources of firewood for the winter which lay ahead; or to find out where interesting crustaceans lived so that we could practise gastronomy; or, perhaps, to find the soft-sand beaches which would allow us to lay our boat over and scrub the hull – careening, as sailors say. It was whilst careening one day that we discovered that whatever you may think, you are never alone.

Doing everything under sail is fun. Our sails filled their bellies with late summer breeze; we felt the deck heel slightly, and then begin to pick up speed over the flat water of the Loch. To both our left and our right was the shore. Three miles ahead lay the open sea; we turned left, for the shore. The brimming high tide on which we floated was depositing yet more bits of seaweed and twigs to add to a collection it kept in a thin brown line at the top of the beach – even from out here we could smell it healthily putrefying.

Mid loch, the depth-sounder had shown more than 20 metres, but now began to fall. We'd done this dozens of times before in all sorts of places, yet it didn't matter – there was always something awful about watching the depth sounder fall, mechanically. Click, and another metre was lost – it seemed to ask if we were sure we wanted to go on with this. By the time the depth had fallen to just three metres we were still a long way off the shore. Grounding out here would be humiliating if anyone happened to come past. But for the next hundred yards, closing ever with the shore, the log didn't shave a millimetre off its report.

The view along our bowsprit was always a variation on the theme of blue water, but began now to fill with the greens and browns of land until at last, with the grey pebbles of beach right under us – it seemed – and the sails softly filled, there was a thump. The bow lifted, the boat stopped dead, we stumbled forward a step, steadied ourselves with a discreet movement from one hand, and knew we were hard aground on a sandy bottom.

We'd chosen the spot the previous day for its sandiness just below the high-water mark, but also for its seclusion because whenever we do something reckless we prefer to do it in private – it saves so much embarrassment if everything goes belly-up. Here seemed *very* private. Among the green hills in Scotland there's always a bothy, a wee croft, or a lonely white cottage with a red tin roof. Here there was nothing, the hills were empty, without even the white dot of a sheep upon them.

The tide began to fall, marooning us until evening. It is now – before the tide has left us, yet whilst we are firmly aground and cannot return to sea – that we are in greatest danger. Left to her own devices our boat will stand upright on her keel like a stork on one leg. A puff of wind catching the lofty mast, once the tide had gone out, would be enough to topple her; she'd fall on the hard wet sand, and the hull would be stove-in. So during this brief window of opportunity we rush around, sweat on our brow. We tie a rope to the top of the mast, row away in the dinghy with its other end, anchor it, and then dangle our weight on the suspended rope in an attempt to pull her off-balance whilst there is still enough water around the hull to give her a soft landing when she falls. We've never failed to get her over, but there have been several occasions when we *wondered* if we would.

Scrubbing the hull took two or three hours and although there was nothing now to 'do', there was plenty to see and hear with all the interesting noises that constantly interrupted the silence. The heavy splash of a fish leaping from the water; a bird calling, territorially; the buzz of a winged insect as it flew past our ears – even a zephyr of wind arriving and scattering the plume of blue smoke rising from our fire seemed filled with interest.

We were smoking an eel over a campfire we'd lit on the stones of our deserted beach. Linda was doing all the hard work as usual – poking it with a stick and chucking on lumps of the weird-looking fuel we'd found in the foothills of the mountains which surrounded us, dried rooty masses shaped like pineapples but as light as shuttlecocks, parched by the dry summer. And she was boiling a kettle to make tea. All we had planned for the afternoon was to watch the kettle boil several times, and to drink the several cups of tea it made. Actually Linda doesn't drink tea – preferring plain boiled water – but it didn't matter, the water in the lochs hereabouts was the *colour* of tea, and wanted a *lot* of boiling. When we went to get our water from a pool which was fed by a crashing waterfall we disturbed an adder that had managed to get half a water-rat in his mouth and was struggling to swallow the rest. Seeing us he realised he'd be unable to bite us with his mouth full, so spat it out and then slithered into the undergrowth leaving the wet-furred corpse of the rat on the bank of the pool. From there it was a logical extrapolation to consider the kind of wildlife which must be *in* the peaty water, and which we *couldn't* see – and who knows but *that* wildlife might be feasting on the rotting carcass of a drowned sheep?

As we waited for the kettle Linda and I sat admiring the view – multi-tasking is nothing to us. The afternoon yawned out before us and not a man or mouse threatened to interrupt our contemplation... or so we thought. Lying on the beach next to us, on its side just below the high-water mark was our boat, and that boat was like a people-magnet.

First we spoke to a group who waded along at the water's edge wearing green PVC dungarees which came up to their armpits. Two were marine biologists carrying clipboards and biros. They wore heavy frowns as though working in paradise was a burden to them. The other two were islanders come along to lend some muscle to the operation – they cast a pair of net curtains repeatedly into the shallow water, retrieved them again, and then poked their heads among the folds of material to see what they'd caught. They were hoping to get some salmon fry so that the biologists could give that species a big tick on their papers and record it as 'present' in the area, but they hadn't found any.

Then a Rigid Inflatable Boat came hurtling into view, banking steeply as it entered the loch from the nameless stretch of sea outside, its engine screaming like an industrial sewing machine. A couple of minutes later, arriving opposite us with the engine noise so loud you couldn't hear yourself think, it spotted us, cut its engine, and pootled toward the low water shore. A landing-party got out: a man of about ninety with two sticks; a woman of similar age who hitched up a tweed skirt, daring to show her ankles and her Queen Anne legs; and another man, much younger – a stiff military type of about sixty, who declined help from the boatman and slid from the inflatable tubes, falling all-fours onto the wet sand. He got up and turned to show his companions the four sandy patches on his knees and elbows with a forced chuckle, but they had turned to look the other way – preserving his dignity, pretending they hadn't noticed him fall. Whilst the boatman stayed on board, polishing glass dials with a finger, the three companions wandered off in different directions. It struck me as rather *un*companionable, and I wondered if they'd had a tiff and would rather find a way to *walk* home than spend another minute in each other's company.

The military man swept the beach with his gaze, in reconnaissance, marched barefoot up to us, folded his hands behind his back, stood at ease, and then began firing questions at us – supplying their answers before we could speak:

'What's going on? – had an accident I s'pose. Much damage done? – probably not – it's a soft beach.' He bobbed up and down to try the sand with his weight. 'Will you be stuck long? – not too long I shouldn't think... the tide's turned now.'

When he'd finished answering his questions, and seemed satisfied with the answers he'd got, he bobbed up and down again on the sand and threw his head back to gaze among the hills, as though he'd joined a queue for a bus. We asked him where he'd come from but the vague stammered answer led us to conclude that it was a military secret. In lieu of an answer he gave us other information which wasn't – he began explaining to us all that we could see around us, parcelling it up for us into easily digestible nuggets as-and-when they occurred to him.

'Lot of deer in those hills – unbelievable amount.'

'Ticks, too – full of Lyme's disease... Have to be careful. Filthy beasts.'

His roving eye found the scientists: 'They won't catch anything there – far too shallow.'

They'd continued their work up the loch and were just about to disappear around the corner.

'Complete waste of time – they don't even look like proper... people.'

Linda and I fly to the defence of anyone who has been misunderstood. We can't help it – the injustice of it excites urgent sympathies within us and, who knows, we might be misunderstood ourselves one day.

'They're biologists... looking for salmon fry,' we told him.

'Mm? Are they? Well, there then! I told you they weren't proper people.'

The biologists had slipped from view. The landing party returned to their boat and its engine whined them back out to sea from whence they came.

The afternoon wore lazily on. Through the steam which rose lazily from my smoky tea as I placed it to my lips I noticed, far off in the distance, the figure of a man half-walking half-running down the hill and onto the beach. He was the only thing that moved in a wide landscape. He stopped to take off his shoes and roll up his trouser legs, stuffed a hand nonchalantly into his pocket, turned in our direction and set off at a casual stroll. Another visitor... things were getting a bit busy round here.

Loch Tarbert is one of the most remote sea lochs on the west coast of Scotland. The scenery is unbelievably pretty: from where we sat a strip of blue water was fringed with white-sand beaches on either side and stretched out in the direction of the sun falling toward the horizon, dazzling us every time we looked west. At the high-water mark the sandy beaches give way first to pebbles, each the size of a melon, then to the impossibly green slopes for which Scotland is famous, and which form the foothills of what anywhere else in the world would be known as mountains – here they are Bheins. Following the craggy outline of the biggest Bhein, up until green fades to brown, ever higher, you notice that the needle of its summit has just pierced a cotton-wool cloud, and is holding it there in exactly the right spot to complete the chocolate-box landscape.

Non boat-owners have a circuitous journey from the mainland to get here: they have to catch a ferry to another island first – then it's a 25-mile drive to a second, smaller ferry, which is a sort of floating car park for eight vehicles with a little conning tower set off to one side. Happily the floating car park is equipped with a gutsy engine capable of mastering the fierce tides which even as they wait are churning past the windscreen. In bad weather – if the skipper has decided to 'chance' a crossing at all – he advises drivers to wind down the windows of their vehicles. At first this seems like some Highland joke – horizontal rain is lashing across the windscreen so hard that the wipers can't cope – and they're about to be inundated by the further addition of bath loads of saltwater every time the car park plunges into a trough... but what the skipper diplomatically avoids mentioning is that with the windows open passengers will be able to escape from their vehicle if the ferry goes down.

Five minutes later, arriving at the other side, half the cars in the car park refuse to start, and the rest begin to limp toward the ramp like dazed animals leaving the Ark. The squiffy little road onto which they emerge looks like someone's driveway except that it's 30 miles long, and a sign-post helpfully points in the only direction available. Forty minutes drive o'er dale and hill, followed by a further two hours on foot, and here you are. Welcome to Loch Tarbert. The island of Jura is 40 miles long, and home to 200 people – none of whom live in this bit.

As the figure neared us we could see he was dark haired, about forty, and had something on his mind. During the final hundred metres or so of his approach, he slowed to an indifferent saunter, making little excursions to the left and to the right to visit interesting-looking pieces of seaweed which had become stranded on the wet sand, or to turn over empty shells with his toes. Arriving close at hand he lifted his head, stopped, and let out a little gasp of surprise to let us know that he hadn't spotted us until that very moment, and that only the wiles of chance had deposited us and our boat in his path.

The attraction we presented to a man who we learned hadn't seen another living soul since breakfast time was that after a long and meandering walk he was the first person to discover a shipwreck and two survivors. His day spent amongst the hills had not now been wasted.

With rolled-up grey worsted trousers, casual jacket – socks bulging in one pocket – and a pair of black brogues swinging in his hand, he looked as though he was off to a matinée as soon as he had rendered us the help we needed. He spoke quietly with the rustic vowels of West Yorkshire.

'Everything all right?'

'Fine, thanks!'

That didn't seem to be the answer he expected and he stood there for a moment blinking at us, as if he'd walked on to a stage, spoken his opening line, and then realised he'd forgotten what came next. He looked to the wings for a prompt.

'How are *you* doing?' we asked.

'Yeah, I'm all right... I am,' he said, wishing there had been a bit more to it than that. He found another shell and turned it over with his toes. It was a tricky operation, but when it had been successfully completed he looked up with a matter-of-fact expression, as though finding a shipwreck was something that had happened *fairly* frequently in his life, but still had the power to add a faint glow of interest if the day had otherwise been uneventful. He tossed his head in the direction of the disaster.

'How did that happen, actually?'

'What?'

'The boat... you know – the boat crash.'

We do this every couple of months – so that we can scrub off any weed or barnacles and check the mechanical gear, see if we've sustained any damage from the numerous underwater collisions we've experienced. We explained this to him. He was unable to hide his disappointment.

'I'd offer to show you around on board,' said Linda, 'but everything is leaning over at 45 degrees ... you can't even stand in it!'

'No – you're all right.'

We felt we'd let him down and to be honest boats *are* more interesting when they've crashed. We all turned our backs on it and pretended it wasn't there.

'What brings you to Jura?'

'Whisky!' he told us.

He was staying in a B&B at Craighouse – the principal settlement, three hours away over the hill. He'd had a tour of the distillery yesterday, woken up late, and had been wandering this way and that 'to clear his head' since ten in the morning and ended up here.

'Where are we, anyway? I didn't bring a *map*,' he said, with a hint that maps were for sissies.

'Loch Tarbert.'

'Oh!' he said, and seemed quite pleased to have arrived somewhere called Loch Tarbert. 'What's the best way back to Craighouse?'

Linda had been reading up on walks on Jura. The book she had was the only guidebook we'd ever read that devoted itself to just two walks, but neither of them came anywhere near here. Jura's road could *count* as a footpath, making 'three' – in fact you could pitch a tent on it for a week and not be in anyone's way. But the road wasn't anywhere near here, either.

'Your best bet would be to retrace your steps,' Linda suggested.

'Yeah well, I *started out* on a path... but it just sort of disappeared.'

'Evan's Walk?'

'That were it! It fizzled out after a couple of miles, and I haven't found it since.'

'What time are they expecting you back?'

'About seven. What time is it now? I haven't got a watch.' Watches are for sissies, too.

'Twenty-past five... you know, you really ought to start back now, it'll be dark by the time you get there...'

'It'll be all right.' He walked around in a little circle looking for more shells to turn and when he didn't find any concluded that his work here was done. He smiled, raised a hand, called a cheerful farewell, and then receded into the distance just as he had arrived – nonchalantly at first, building speed, until we saw his urgent silhouette in the west like a hill-runner. I hope he made it, but we never heard whether he did or not – he was the last person we saw for a fortnight.

2 MAROONED IN A BLIZZARD

LINDA AND I PREFER THE NICE BITS OF SAILING and leave the hardships of wild ocean passages to others better suited to that kind of thing. But we inshore sailors carry on our hobby along coasts which present, if anything, more dangers than the open sea, and it was sobering as we passed the jagged teeth which form the north coast of Islay to remember that that was where the *Exmouth* went down. If loss of life at sea can be ranked into descending layers of abysmal tragedy – and even folk who live far from the sea are shocked by shipwrecks – then the loss of life when the *Exmouth* struck the rocks surely reaches down to the pit-bottom of horror, if only because most of the 'souls' on board *were* women and children.

Having met a storm on her way to Canada – sailing from Ireland with immigrants hoping to make a new life in Quebec in 1837 – the *Exmouth* turned back with most of her sails blown out, rendering her virtually uncontrollable. She foundered on the coast of Islay with the loss of 220 lives and so violent was the sea that dashed itself onto those rocks that she broke up in less than ten minutes. 108 bodies were recovered, mostly limbless, headless or faceless; 72 of them children under the age of fourteen. In those days – the days of tall ships – the first instinct of the sailors aboard who knew what they were about, and could see that their ship would founder, was to climb the rigging and tie themselves in it. Oftentimes when a ship is lost it's in relatively shallow water and many's the tall ship that has sunk below the waves leaving her masts, for a time, above. Three crewmembers climbed the masts of the *Exmouth* and hung in the rigging watching their ship break up beneath them. When the rigging parted, the masts collapsed, throwing them ashore. They were the only survivors.

Wyre Majestic – a more recent casualty on Islay's shores

As the summer season grew old and the days became shorter our excursions became fewer. We'd sail over seas which seemed to be slowing down in preparation for winter; the air which filled our sails seemed more solid, heavier and – looking into the distance – clearer. The waters flowing around the islands on the West Coast of Scotland – which are never busy with yachts – soon cleared of them altogether; instead we had for company, as we nosed from place to place, slow-moving – almost fixed – scallop dredgers (the clam boats) dotted around us on the horizon. Closer inshore, crabbers rushed from place to place, tiny boats pushing great bow waves ahead of them, and having arrived at their pot-buoys they'd stop for an hour to empty their fleets of pots, re-bait them, and shoot them once more down to the rocks below, many fathoms deep.

The breeze across our deck became colder, the sails stiffer, the sea greyer, and our intention as we sailed over it these days was always to arrive quickly at our destination so that we'd be settled on our anchor well before darkness, which arrived noticeably earlier every day. We kept the wood-burning stove permanently alight. Stepping down below from the pinching wind either on a passage or at anchor was the most cheerful feeling in the world. It was cosy. It was home.

We were committed to a Scottish winter, and in any case it was too late in the year to leave. Instead of running for cover with everyone else at the first sign of an autumn gale – to the security of a marina, or to the tropical blue-waters and swaying palm trees of Cornwall – we had decided to spend a whole winter up here to discover the hard way if man could 'survive' the cold, and the fierce winter storms, alone on a boat among the sparse and often uninhabited sea lochs. I mentioned at the close of my last book, *Phoenix from the Ashes*, that we'd just completed some film work, and looked forward to the winter ahead – it is from there that I take up the tale now.

We'd made the final decision to try a Scottish winter back in the soft days of summer when you can't remember what 'winter' is like, and imagine that it 'won't be too bad'. It must be encoded into human mitochondria that we can't remember how cold winter gets and gives us all the courage to face another. Because we couldn't remember what it was like we welcomed it with bubbles of anticipation, and imagined that it would be an unforgettable experience – which it was, as it happened, but for different reasons. And we imagined, too, that spending a winter in Scotland would give us a chance to get to know the place like natives, in all its moods.

Linda is a Glaswegian, so I aimed at her all my questions about how to prepare, and what we should be looking out for. But she'd moved away from Glasgow at the age of four or five, she said, and couldn't remember much about the place. Then, brightening, having just remembered a time she visited her Nan at Largs, and they'd eaten an ice-cream in Nardini's, she told me that it was delicious! But even when I'd heard the long version, got all the facts about that family excursion, and stretched them as far as they would reach, it didn't tell me much about Scotland.

Winter began well enough. Sitting down below decks in late November in the muggy warmth, sketching and listening to music whilst the rain pattered on deck, was enervating. Lying snugly to our anchor in a loch which was well-protected from the heaving sea outside we'd catch each other's eye occasionally for the sole purpose of exchanging contented smiles as much as to say: *Isn't this wonderful? What fun we're having!*

Living in a house which rolls a bit has been clinically-proven to be better for you than living in a house which doesn't: it's life-affirming, they say, and produces feelings of happiness and vitality. The wind sang in the rigging, and we snubbed gently to the left then to the right as our boat chawed at her anchor. On deck, our 12-volt wind generator would hum occasionally in a gust to remind us that it was stuck out there, cold, miserable, and busily working to provide us with our mood lighting for the evening.

By December it began to rain hard, and endlessly – well, not literally *endlessly*... sometimes it would stop raining and start to snow. The Bheins by which we were surrounded seemed to catch lofty snow clouds which might otherwise have passed harmlessly overhead, and funnel them down to us. We'd watch the first flurries way up on the mountaintops, a fluttering white hem of skirts passing lightly over the summit, then sweeping down their slopes drawing a white veil over the blacks, browns and purples of the rock, miraculously smudging them out like an eraser over the soft-whiteness of a landscape-artist's paper, removing all his work as though everything behind the snow storm had expired, ceased to be. Moments later it reached the shore, spotted us out at anchor, and came dancing lightly across the water to remove us too. As it reached us the air, which could hardly be described as warm, became as chilly as death, and we were gone.

Our world now consisted only of the wet-dark wood of our deck shining through the melt water of fallen snow, and the tiny allowance of steel-grey sea on which we floated. Beyond that, within a few metres, all was white.

We pushed the hatch closed – it made a different sound in the snow – and dropped in the wash boards which sealed us from the outside world. Then we settled down to spend another day in the gloomy half-light of our boat.

When you're stuck below decks, week after week – not daring to step outside for fear of getting soaked through, numbed with hypothermia, then slipping off the icy deck and drowning – the pleasure of life aboard begins to pall. We felt sorry for ourselves, and envious of people who live in houses.

We keep about 300 kilos of dry firewood on board. That's about ten or twelve 'feed' sacks of logs, which lasts us for two or three weeks. It was beginning to run low, so as soon as a day arrived on which we could stick our heads out of the hatch and describe the weather as only 'miserable', I loaded the chainsaw and wood-splitting maul into the dinghy, bent my waxed coat – which was stiff with cold in the wet-locker – into a shape which would accept my body, and fitted myself into its tubes. It was an old coat. Atomic decay had caused it to lose its Driza-boneness in all the areas where it was most needed so the previous winter I had had the brainwave of drowning it in Waxoyl – a car-care product used for extending the life of old bangers on which rust is causing the paint to blister. The coat stinks, but Waxoyl is a demon for keeping out the water, and there's not a flake of rust on it.

It was a chore to row ashore through occasional showers of sleet and then spend half a day poking about in the wet forest. What we look for are long-dead – and therefore 'seasoned' – trees which are either still standing, or which have fallen but have somehow contrived to stay above the ground rather than coming into contact with it, usually by falling into the branches of another tree. Even after a prolonged wet spell like this one, although the outside may be wet, inside the wood will be dry and ring out like a bell if you strike it. As they say in Devon, *You get 'yet'* (hot) *twice* felling your own firewood; dragging it to the shore, sawing it into rounds, and then splitting it with a maul. Four hours later I was sweating as if it were a summer's day, and wondering how on earth all my piles of split logs would fit into a dinghy which was designed to be small enough to fit on deck, primarily, and for haulage secondarily. Someone once described it as a cockleshell – a remark which so wounded me that whenever I row ashore for firewood, even in remote places where no one can see me, I demonstrate to an absent audience how much my cockleshell can carry, and overload it perilously.

In went 300 kilos of firewood, the chainsaw, the splitting maul, and I sat on top of the wood pile like an early Christian martyr. The water across which I had to row was smooth; a ripple would have sunk us.

As I pulled on the oars and the distance between me and the shore began to grow, I heard a splash just behind me – just in front of the boat as I was facing backwards – and turned to look for what I imagined would be a seal banging its tail on the water in protest as it disappeared below the surface. They do that presumably to let you know that you are intruding on their territory. Yet I saw nothing at all and so continued to row until something caught my eye in my wake: through the crystal water of the loch I was shocked to see a piece of orange plastic rubbish lying on the sea bed. How could someone visit such unspoiled beauty and chuck rubbish into the water, I asked myself, and became increasingly incensed at the mindless vandalism of it as I sculled.

It was only when I began to wonder what the piece of rubbish had been that it occurred to me that both the shape and colour of it were reminiscent of a chainsaw, and with that turned to look over my shoulder to check that my own saw was still safely wedged between bags – yet in its place saw only an empty space where my chainsaw once had been. At that point it occurred to me that a coincidence was brewing here.

Getting my saw back from the bottom of the loch nearly cost me my life: I leant over to reach into the icy water with my bare arm – poking at the saw with an oar which I was trying to insert through the moulded handle – when the sound of rushing water brought my attention to the fact that the gunwale of my dinghy was submerged, and was drinking greedily at the loch water. Getting the saw to work again was merely the employment of a day-and-a-half – and yet people ask us how we 'fill' our time living on board a boat. If they would only follow us attentively for an hour we'd show them how naturally the completion of one small task requires the setting-up of a dozen industries to support it. Two hours and they'd wonder we didn't employ staff.

Now that the lazarette was stuffed full of wood it became apparent that the weather had been waiting for this moment to get worse and added a hard gale to the freezing temperatures.

If there were any leaves remaining on the trees before the gale, there were none afterwards. That gale, after a short lull, was followed by another more severe, and then a third.

Throughout all this our boat chomped on its anchor chain like a nervous horse on its bit, weaving from side to side. The water in which we floated was streaked with foam, yet thankfully, because it was shallow and the shore was nearby, the waves were denied the chance to grow above a foot or two. All the same, what waves there were dashed themselves against our hull with a slap and sent spray across the deck. By day and by night our boat gently lifted and shimmied like a fairground ride which no one could remember how to switch off. The hull became a sound-box for the stringed-instrument of our moaning steel rigging, which whined to each new blast, rising in tone in the violent gusts to such a shriek that it stopped us from what we were doing and made us look up at the deck-head – as if we'd learn something by looking there – and our eyes would meet, each checking the other to see if we were 'worried' by this new development. Very occasionally two or three lengths of rigging sounded together to make a chord, or discord, so grating, so troublesome to the soul and vexatious to the spirit that it reminded me of the time Linda was learning the violin. We put on a brave face, but after days of it our nerves were raw. Our ship became a prison and whenever its inmates' eyes met, they met joylessly, staring out from expressionless faces. It was unnecessary to talk about how we were feeling – we could *see* how we were feeling.

The phone rang. It almost never rang because there was almost never a signal. I blinked at it for so long I nearly missed the call. It was John, ringing from Cornwall.

'Just a quick call – only idle chat,' he announced cheerfully as the usual prelude to an hour's blathering.

I went on deck without stopping to pull on a coat or woolly hat. The wind blew snowflakes onto my cheeks, burning them, and when it had melted and my cheek was wet, the icy wind cut deeper. We don't have any awnings. The best shelter I could find was by standing in the shadow of the pole-mast.

'Justin! We've had a *load* of bloody firewood delivered this afternoon so we're sitting here, Pam and I, in our T shirts, would you believe... in front of a blazing fire... though God knows we don't need it, it's so *mild* isn't it? We're building up a real fug in here!'

He and I laughed involuntarily at their surfeit.

'Anyway, we were just sipping a glass of Glayva – my favourite whisky liqueur, as you know – and it made us think of you all the way up there in Scotland, so we thought we'd give you a quick call and find out how you're getting on – how's things?'

'Great thanks!'

'What's the weather doing with you?'

'Well, it's cold. Snowing. Blizzard, actually... with all this wind.'

'Snow you say?'

'Yes.'

'Oh God, Justin! I bet that's pretty... on the hills and everything?'

'Can't see the hills, John... it's snowing too heavily. And anyway, it's dark.'

'Dark?! Already?'

'Yes.' I swapped hands to hold the phone with the warm one. I looked down and saw that the front of my jumper had a snow bib glued to it. I slipped a hand under my jumper and attempted to shake it free, but it only cracked the snow and made room for more. You don't need to contribute much to the conversation once John has found his gear so I stood and listened, cold as a Humboldt penguin. John changed the subject to something more interesting – he's a precision engineer and likes to talk about what he's been doing in his workshop. It's not that I'm not interested in Engineering, I am – sort of. But the difference between John and me is the difference between a skilled mechanic and someone who knows how to open the bonnet.

'Justin, I was talking to a bloke today and he had an old Cummins 11 A – not the *noo* version, the *old* one – a real workhorse... with the reciprocating fuel scavenger. D'you know the one I mean?'

'No.'

'Well, listen to this because you'll be interested in this. When I was about seventeen – or I might have been eighteen – say seventeen-and-a-half cos it doesn't matter anyway... I knew a bloke who had a dog, a right bloody-old mongrel, it was...'

Half an hour later, when he'd rounded up that story, he went on to tell me the 20lb pollock story: 'I know I'm repeating myself here...' he said. 'I've told you this story loadsa times before...' Then he gave another airing to the story about driving to Rome in an HGV with his mate and 30 tons of oysters – or they might have been prawns, or perhaps they were peas – and the refrigeration unit broke down during a heatwave, and when they got there they had 30 tons of maggots. And then finally he told me the one about winning a bet by doing a 400yd wheelie, blindfolded, across a ploughed field on a Motocross bike which had only one wheel – the front one – whilst eating a Cornish pasty with his feet. I didn't stop him. I shivered through all of them, until my head had turned blue, because it was nice just to hear John's voice.

John

I climbed back down below decks and sat next to the fire, holding my hands over it without feeling anything. Linda was rolling out some oatcakes. I broke the silence.

'The days are short and dark; it only stops raining to snow; the nearest decent supermarket is three days away regardless of how you get there; our boat is like a bloody prison – but if I set all that to one side, I don't believe I've ever been happier in my life.'

I thought of John and Pam in front of their fire in mild Cornwall, dazzled by the late afternoon sunshine streaming through an open window. 'They'll be on the phone next week to tell us the bloody daffodils are up,' I said.

The prospect of Christmas didn't help. It was gloomy to imagine that this is what it would be like on Christmas Day. Then I had a brainwave and banged my hand down on the table making the oatcakes jump. Linda looked at me with a face as long as a funeral bell.

'Got it! Let's phone up the Chesworths and ask if we can spend the winter in their holiday cottage. Now – whilst we've still got a signal!'

An ember of hope kindled in her eyes.

'It'll be great!' I went on. 'We'll book the boat into a marina up here... I'll find work in sunny old Cornwall to pay for it... then in the spring we'll come back, chip our boat out of the ice, and sail away south, never to return. They've got a wood-burner there, you know... And a telly! And they said we could spend the winter in it anytime!'

She needed no persuading so I wrapped myself against the blizzard, climbed on deck, and retraced my footprints through the snow to the mast and dialled their number. Just *phoning* Cornwall made me feel warmer. I waited nervously to see if the phone would be picked up. It was.

'Blimey!' said Mr Chesworth. 'Have you reached the Pole?'

'The Pole would be warmer.'

'Are you surviving?'

'Barely... it's bloody freezing, Chessie, and we were wondering if there was any chance of us coming down to stay in the holiday cottage for a couple of months?' Just then – it may have been the cold, or it may have been nerves – my teeth chattered involuntarily. Whatever caused it, it was perfectly timed. The question was followed by a long silence that doesn't usually precede a positive answer. I looked at the phone – three bars.

'Hello?' I said.

Eventually Peter spoke: 'Here's Terri...'

There was another pause before I heard his wife come on the phone. 'Well, I don't know why he's passed the phone to me...'

It must have been hard to break the news, but as gently as she could she explained that it was already let. When she'd finished, Peter came back on the phone.

'You could have it next year..?' he suggested.

I slumped next to the fire.

'Did you get through?' Linda asked.

I nodded.

Neither of us spoke for an hour.

We considered the possibility of sailing the 500 miles back to the milder south. Our boat isn't really very practical for just the two of us; we built her filled with romantic nostalgia and some of our gear is over-sized and heavy – too heavy for Linda who's really just a tiny thing, and a *bit* heavy for me, confidentially, when the wind gets up. There are acres of sail-cloth, heavy wooden spars, miles of rope – and our sailing, steering and anchoring is all done by hand. She's difficult to get going, harder to stop, and someone has to be on deck every inch of the way without any protection from wind and spray. In the summer, it's pleasant; in the winter we might not survive. We decided to stay in Scotland and mug it out.

Then something strange happened: the weather began to improve, our hibernation ended and before Christmas we were back, moving around again. Although the days were short the weather was settled. The sun shone with pale brilliance, picking out the dazzling white tops of mountains, just as it picked out the dazzling white tops of waves which raced across the Sound, or dashed themselves onto walls of smooth yellow rock. Close inshore, the heads of otters and seals glinted in the sun as they bobbed to the surface in the swell, then dived again into the kelp far below.

John MacArthur from the Ardfern Yacht Club, noticing that we were live-aboards, realised that we must have a story to tell and invited us to speak at one of their winter-evening meetings. I get nervous speaking in public, particularly when I haven't rehearsed, so Linda tactfully left me alone on board the day before the event to deliver the talk to myself, get used to the sound of my own voice, and make my mistakes in private.

When we walked through the car park to the village hall where the talk was to be held we noticed that it was packed. At first I hoped that this meant the hall had been double-booked with a WI sale of homemade preserves and that I wouldn't be needed after all. But it soon became clear they had generously turned out in their 'tens' on this winter evening to hear our story.

'Are you nervous?' Linda asked. When I thought about it I realised that I knew the subject pretty well – and if I made a mistake, who was there to call me a liar?

'Funnily enough, no,' I said.

In the event, of course, far from trying my evidence forensically the audience was eager and attentive. For dramatic effect I began by describing how we'd lost our house in a fire, followed that with our decision to build a wooden boat as amateurs starting with the trees, and described (briefly) how we went about building it, before settling down to concentrate on the day-to-day trivia of our life on board.

It was during that stretch of the talk that things really took off. What began as murmurs of delight soon developed to become thigh-slapping laughs, and before I knew where I was people were sliding from their chairs to the floor in convulsions of laughter and having to be helped to their feet. As I stood there on stage, baffled by how well it was all going, it struck me that the audience thought I was mad, and things had got so bad that I could scarcely open my mouth without the audience fancying they saw some joke in it.

I remember telling them: 'We have a wood-burning stove and fell trees for firewood wherever we happen to be anchored – but perhaps the least said about that the better...'

That simple observation was followed by another explosion of laughter. Five people had to be carried out of the room by St John's Ambulance, who were themselves gasping for breath and clutching at the air, which left the rest of the audience on the floor clinging to the legs of their chairs for support, rocking with uncontrollable mirth. By the time the talk was over we'd made fifty new friends and were practically carried on their shoulders to the bar of the Galley of Lorne Inn.

3 A BROKEN BOWSPRIT

LINDA SAYS SHE DOESN'T HAVE MANY REGRETS about selling the house to live on board a boat, but the things she misses most are a washing machine, a bath, and somewhere to store her shoes. And she grudges the fact that the neatly folded jumpers, shirts and trousers for which there *are* spaces on board always have about them a faint whiff of paraffin, and some bore-dust from the woodworm we hear when we're in bed some nights, dining at our expense.

Shortly after we launched our boat we were invited for a cup of tea on board another newly-launched self-built boat of a similar length to ours by a cheerful couple planning to go to the 'Med'. *Their* boat had all the things Linda missed. It was based on Joshua Slocum's boat, *Spray*, which he famously sailed around the world single-handedly, starting in 1895. Theirs was a steel version of his boat, weighed a ton – well, more than a ton of course – and was as big as a warehouse when you went down below. I believe it had its own echo. It certainly had a bath, a washing machine *and* an oil-fired Rayburn – a Rayburn for heaven's sake! – which made it as warm as toast. Too warm, really. Their boat reminded me of a swish flat I'd once been to view in Cheltenham with the intention of renting it.

Their Spray was at anchor on one of those chilly-but-dry autumn days which send little wavelets trilling across Falmouth Harbour until they become lost from view under the pier-legs of the dock. I remember when we climbed down the companionway steps to meet Mrs Spray for the first time we interrupted her doing the ironing. Our arrival couldn't have come at a better time, she said, untying her apron; on the one hand she was only too pleased for a break from the ironing, and on the other our admiration of her Rayburn – we'd been staring at it open-mouthed since arriving, unable to take another step – reminded her that she'd got some meringues in the oven which were due out about now. I popped my head out of the hatch to glimpse the horizon and know I wasn't in a dream. I never thought I'd get Linda off that boat – and she doesn't even eat meringue. Heavy boats are slow boats, I told her when I eventually managed to get her home – that Rayburn's half a ton by itself. And as for all that Le Creuset...

My only slither of consolation came a few weeks later when we were watching the Sprays sail out of Falmouth on the first leg of their journey toward the Med and noticed they were being overtaken by an oil rig which had somehow slipped its mooring. But, there, that shows me in a bad light: speed isn't everything. And in any case, that was four years ago – I expect they'll be halfway across the channel by now.

For a whole month afterwards the artificiality of their boat made me ashamed of the simple life we led. So I worked hard to gloss-over any shortcomings our boat might have: every morning I ran Linda's bath for her – well, I say *bath*... I half-filled a hand-basin with steaming water from the kettle and set it on a fluffy towel within the deliciously warm glow of our wood-burning stove – not *too* close since the morning she bent to wash her face and branded herself with the words *Aarrow Stoves*, one per cheek. I know you can't lie down full-length and 'soak' in a hand-basin, but the fresh water we carry in our tanks, used thus sparingly, lasts weeks at a time and frees us from the slavery of always being near civilisation, and a marina tap. Having said all that, when we built our boat we included a generous-sized wet-room opposite the loo – I mention this just in case the Sprays are listening – *and* it's supplied with pressurised hot water, lashings of the stuff. But we've never used it for fear of the boat mouldering, becoming fetid and upsetting the woodworm.

If Linda's day doesn't begin with a pot of freshly percolated coffee she becomes indifferent to whether she lives or dies. So

I make coffee and chuck a few doorsteps of home-baked bread on the flat-top of the wood-burning stove and pretty soon the boat becomes filled with the mouth-watering smell of hot buttered toast and coffee. We're so *homely* on board at times that I half-expect to get an estate agent's flyer some mornings asking if we're thinking of selling because they've got a cash-buyer urgently seeking to move to the area.

Every so often we spend a day or two back in civilisation to socialise, shop, and take long showers. With the latter in mind, and an invitation to lunch from some new friends we'd met, we returned to Ardfern Marina. It's so well protected at the top of Loch Craignish that some boats were overwintering on their moorings, dozing next to their limp hawsers. We entered the marina through a gap in the pontoons, circled left until we were about-face, then reversed neatly into a space without hitting anything – thereby saving ourselves millions of pounds.

Our bowsprit

Our bowsprit is built like a tree – it *is* a tree – so it came as a surprise when we returned from one of our shore visits to find it snapped in two. It was just before Christmas and we'd returned from our lunch with Mike and his partner Suzanne. We met Mike a couple of months earlier when he was standing together with Graham (the same 'Gypsy' Graham I spoke of in *Phoenix*) alongside our boat doing what everyone does who gives our boat a second glance – staring up at its mast. Late-forties, short, and with a well-trimmed black beard, he faced you square-on when he talked, but even so you had to listen carefully because he was very softly spoken. He wore a blue blazer with brass buttons – I noticed it particularly because they're not very fashionable these days – which made it easy to guess at his background. Too thin to be a coach driver and too young to play lawn-bowls, that jacket left me in no doubt that he'd been a naval officer – reinforced by the fact that he stood with one hand behind his back. I discovered that I was correct in my assumption when he mentioned that he'd served on board the Royal Yacht *Britannia*. And he was correct in his assumption about me when he asked me if I'd ever heard of it.

Mike and Suzanne had just moved to Scotland from Hounslow, where they lived under the flight path to Heathrow Airport, citing that as their main reason for moving away. From their bedroom window they could see how much tread there was left on the tyres of the incoming jets which arrived every 90 seconds.

'And loads of planes dump fuel before landing, you can taste it in the air, and see it on the cars and the roofs of houses.'

By the time he'd finished describing their street you felt the next person to light a fag in it would start a fire burning there that would rage for a month.

The only flying craft on view from their window now were herring gulls winging their way across the loch and out toward the Western Isles. We watched them as we picked away at a buffet consisting of everything you see on the trays of a supermarket delicatessen counter but never buy because there are just the two of you.

Mike had bought himself a small wooden yacht which he kept at Ardfern and, as you'd expect from an ex-naval officer, had managed to make the job of repainting its hull last two months. So far. Having said that, the paintwork was immaculate. The reason the job had taken so long was that every day at six bells he'd put the lid back on the paint – a lid which in reality had only just been pulled off – cleaned his brush, and marched into Graham's workshop. Well, I say Graham's *workshop* – it was eight sheets of Stirling board screwed together on a frame of 2x2s, and had a hobbit-hole cut out of it with a jig-saw. As Mike marched in, one arm would be swinging, the other bore a bag of patisseries like a ceremonial mace. He'd fill Graham's kettle and announce that tea would be ready in five minutes. Graham, too, was working on a boat, and from deep in the bowels of it would come the non-committal response of someone not used to being ordered about. Nevertheless, five minutes later on the dot Graham's spindly legs would pick their way over the coaming and down the ladder because the pastries were excellent. The pair of them would stand in the doorway, rocking from heel to toe, blowing the steam off their tea, dropping crumbs onto the gravel, and sympathising with each other about the insurmountable hurdles their morning had presented them with, and offer one another advice on how they might be overcome.

At our Christmas buffet luncheon it was lovely to lounge around chatting in a house for a change, and enjoying such views. So we stayed for several hours, but as we walked back to the boat we noticed immediately that there was something strange about our bowsprit – it wasn't there. At first we quaintly thought that someone might have borrowed it, but when we climbed on board we found half of it was still bolted on deck – the rest had broken off at the 'Gammon Iron', which is that steel hoop at the bow through which the bowsprit pokes its 8-foot nose. Some kind-hearted person had very tidily lashed the broken piece to the side of the deck, twirling its rigging around it like a maypole halfway through a ribbon dance.

We blinked first at it, then at each other. We were at a complete loss to imagine what could have delivered the extreme violence required to break it. Our best guess was that an oil tanker had inadvertently turned into the loch and swiped it as it passed full-steam ahead shortly before running aground.

But there was no tanker. And in any case, whereas you might have expected to see a trail of destruction spread over many miles, only our boat had been singled out for rough-handling.

Just then I noticed a veteran yard-worker stroll down the ramp and onto the pontoon with the unhurried gait of a man trying for redundancy. He fixed us with his eye above unsmiling lips and came on as mechanically as the pendulum of a grandfather clock – even from that distance we knew we were the object of his journey. The curve of his eyebrows, carried high, almost touching his fringe, gave him the appearance of a man who was constantly required to practise tolerance in trying circumstances, as though God had purposed him at birth to help others, whether they deserved it or not. The burden of all that, after long continuance, had diminished the pleasure he derived from his charitable work, and accounted for the grim set of his jaw.

'Have you seen what's happened to your bowsprit?' he demanded.

We *had* seen it, and there was no point in pretending we hadn't.

'Yes,' we admitted.

'I speck you're wondering how it happened?'

We looked at each other to learn whether that was a fair observation of how our thoughts ran.

'Yes,' we said.

His explanation at first seemed less likely than our tanker, and was made all the more unlikely because the day had been so placid, grey and sluggish. He told us that a whirlwind had arrived unexpectedly and from nowhere, raging for almost five minutes. Even his lunchbox had been blown to the ground, he told us, then paused to allow us time to digest this shocking new development. The whirlwind unfurled our sail, inflating it like a parachute. There is far too much cloth in our jib – in anyone's jib – to offer to the kind of wind he described with eyes as round as saucers. He swore it was as true as he was standing there that once he'd gained our deck he'd risked his life to get everything back under control, what with eight feet of tree whizzing about his ears on bits of string. And then – to make his ordeal vivid for us – he performed a one-act play in which King George appeared to be fighting a dragon. We watched open-mouthed, and it was heart-stopping to see the peril he had been in.

Our boat didn't look quite right after that – its nose was crumpled like a paper aeroplane. To make a new bowsprit we'd need to get back to Devon, 600 miles away, to the workshop where we'd built the boat, and which still housed all our tools and timber – but how were we going to get there... or back?

4 GETTING INTO TROUBLE WITH A CHAINSAW

'I USED TO LIVE THERE,' GRAHAM CROAKED. His voice was always croaky – some mornings he could scarcely speak at all. He turned off the engine of his old pick-up truck and it wheezed into silence. Following his gaze through the window of his door, I saw a field gate, and beyond that, a meadow.

We were travelling along one of those roads in the Scottish Highlands which wind through glens for 30 miles to connect two places you've never heard of; countryside so isolated, so far from modern technology – like mobile phone aerials – that the road frequently goes the wrong side of a mountain to take you past the door of a remote farmhouse so that you can pop in and ask to use the phone if you get a puncture.

Now that our bowsprit was broken we were spending an enforced sojourn at the marina. The tip of our bowsprit mounts an important 'stay' for the mast – the mast won't fall down without it, but you durst-not go a-sailing. One of the advantages of our marina holiday was that we could have hot showers every morning; one of the disadvantages – apart from the fact that it was the most expensive marina north of Brighton – was that there were no trees nearby which we could fell for firewood. We'd already run out, and had started to act as the yard's official incinerator for discarded timber. A lot of the wood we were picking up had been painted or varnished – it stank when we burned it, and we'd heard that those sorts of fumes aren't very good for you. Graham offered to drive me to a pile of larch trees he had seasoning in the woods, saw up a load for firewood, and drop them back at our boat.

Graham had just bought himself an old creaker of a timber boat in which he was planning to sail to Hawaii. She was looking a bit sorry for herself: varnish flaking, and with some of her boards blackened at one end – a sure sign that she wouldn't float... or not for very long. Her original owner had fallen behind with payments and never came near. After years of chasing him for the money the marina had sold the boat to recoup its losses. Graham wasn't a sailor, hadn't set foot on board a boat until he'd bought that one, but was at that time of life when you wake up one morning and decide to reinvent yourself. His plan was to sail to Hawaii, a journey so daring in a boat of that size that it needed a lifetime's experience at sea to successfully bring it off – experience he neither possessed, nor was he aware that he didn't possess it. In short, the sort of behaviour we all admire.

At 25ft his boat was ideal for weekends spent exploring the up-river creeks of the East Coast, with a pipe and a bottle of single-malt. It wasn't *unknown* for a boat like his to cross the hundred or so miles of sea which separate England and France – the bit that we, to the intense irritation of the French, call the English Channel – and if the boat makes it to the other side the skipper is sung about for a thousand years whenever people gather around a fire. Very occasionally – perhaps once in a generation – you hear that someone is setting off in one with the intention of sailing it to Hawaii. Their friends and family line the dock, handkerchief in hand, with mixed emotions. On the one hand they know that they will never see him again. On the other... well, on the other it's a bit of a relief – he was always something of a loose cannon, and it's good to see the back of him.

In preparation, throughout the winter, industrious sounds could be heard coming from on board his boat as he worked with a chainsaw and sledgehammer to make her accommodation – to use his own words – 'a bit more stylish'. By night he was studying some books I'd lent him on seamanship and navigation. Or at least I thought he was.

Back in his pick-up truck, I lifted myself out of the soft springs of the passenger seat and craned my neck to see over Graham's head.

'How do you mean you used to *live* there?'

'In my gypsy wagon – it was the first place I stayed when I came to Scotland.'

'Did you have permission?'

'No.'

There was something about Graham that you couldn't help admiring, in spite of yourself. He was fifty-two and had abused drugs all his life – that's why his voice was just a rasping whisper, he told me. He'd given up 'hard' drugs after a near-death experience and now counted himself lucky to be alive – owed his life, in fact, to the NHS. Picking up where they'd left off – and as a tribute to all they had achieved – he now nurtured that life, coaxing it along from one day to the next with the help of carrier bags full of marijuana to gain all its medicinal benefits.

He lived alone in a bow-topped, horse-drawn gypsy caravan which his pony had pulled up to Scotland from Kent – 600 miles away – four years earlier. Inside his wagon were the basic things you need for a simple life: a bed generously piled with ethnic-patterned bedspreads, a wood-burning stove, an oil lamp swinging from a roof hoop, kitchen utensils hanging in rows from hand-carved pegs, woodworking tools, and a set of bagpipes (Northumbrian).

He picked up work here and there, and sold cleverly-thought-out carved-wood furniture to galleries, or made them to order. He'd been trained as a cabinetmaker in the royal household on the Isle of Wight until he fell out with the master craftsman. He worked enough to live, to pay his way, and when he wasn't working – in these, his bonus years... the years after he *didn't* die – his purpose in life was to save the spiritual earth by peaceful meditation, or by militant intervention.

He showed me 'his' meadow: he unlatched the gate, familiarly, and we walked in.

'And you lived out here... all on your own?'

'No – I'd got Jess.'

'Who's Jess?'

'Black lurcher. She was fast... could catch anything. She kept us going.'

'What happened to her?'

'She was old.'

We held a minute's silence in remembrance of her. I could tell by the tone of his voice that he missed her.

'Lovely spot,' I said as we walked down to the bank of a river backed by plump hills.

'Yeah, tis.'

He wasn't really listening. He had his mouth open, and was running his eye slowly along the near horizon as though looking for something. He spoke again, half to himself: 'I wasn't the only one living here...'

'Who else lived here?'

'Fairies.'

'Fairies?'

I stole a glance at him out of the corner of my eye: he was far away, guileless. Nodding softly, he turned to me.

'One night I was playing the chanter of my pipes – just staring into the fire kinda thing – and when I looked up I saw the *King* of the Fairies... standing right in front of me!'

He laughed, as though I'd struggle to believe that bit – as though it still surprised him, even now, that he should have been chosen, honoured.

'How did you know he was the King of the Fairies?'

Every so often I caught a look on Graham's face that I wasn't meant to see. He wouldn't hurt my feelings, but he lost patience with me when I asked a particularly stupid question. He fixed my eye, and allowed his head to fall to one side.

'Cos he was *f—king huge*!'

'Did he say why he'd come?'

'Well, I asked him that, I said to him: *What the f—k do you want*?' (It tickled me to hear how he addressed a king.) 'He just smiled and said: I've come to hear you play.'

Graham impersonated the King – folded his arms, drew himself up to full height, and smiled majestically, his beard parted at the lips, revealing two rows of bad teeth and a dark hole where another used to live. We looked at one another for a few moments. Graham shrugged.

Turning back to the meadow he scanned the horizon again. Eventually he said: 'See that sugar-loaf type of hill over there?'

'Yep.'

'A black dragon lives in there.'

I was about to ask him how he knew, but stopped myself just in time.

Graham

A couple of miles further along the road, we turned onto a forestry track. Graham stopped his truck by a pile of felled larch trees twenty feet long, and all well-seasoned. We got out, breathed in the damp piny air, dragged our chainsaws from the pick-up, fired them up, and shattered the silence into a thousand pieces.

We hadn't been sawing long, bent double, standing on the pile of tree trunks – accumulating a thick layer of freshly cut sawdust on our backs, which fell like snow having been fired into the air by our blades – when to my surprise, through the blizzard, I noticed a pair of slippers on the ground behind me. And not just the slippers – there was someone standing in them. I turned to see a short, slight, dark-haired man in his late thirties, and had the distinct impression that he wished to speak. I switched off my saw and waited for Graham to notice him too. He did. When silence fell, we three stood looking at one another in astonishment until, very calmly, the stranger opened the palms of his hands.

'What are you doing with my trees?'

It's funny. In all the time Linda and I had been living on board, sawing-up trees, I'd been dreading someone asking me that question – yet no one had, until now. I'm not proud of the fact that I take my firewood *without permission* because my mum always told me that taking things without permission was wrong. But we light our wood-burning stove in September and burn it right through until May, consuming three or four tons of firewood – the supply of which is life or death to us.

It's true that we know of one or two people who live on boats in Cornwall who have no heating at all, but during cold spells they don't look as though they're thriving. We see them emerge late-morning, drag themselves about their chores for a few hours then batten down the hatches in the late afternoon, not appearing again until the following day – a sort of part-time hibernation.

So wherever we are, summer or winter, we scan the upper branches of any nearby wood with a pair of binoculars looking for the cream-coloured bald branches of a dead ash tree, or those huge, curvy, splintered branches which Scots pine trees so continually and carelessly drop to the woodland floor. Having spotted our tree, if no one's about I put on a chequered shirt to make myself look like a lumberjack and row quietly ashore. My heart will be pounding, and there'll be beads of sweat upon my brow because I hate confrontation. I know if I can get the *felling* part of the job over with quickly and drag the tree down to the beach I'll feel better because beaches are usually public rights of way, so at least I'll have the law on my side as far as trespassing is concerned. With that question settled, I've got a stack of faultless 'sustainability' arguments to present to any irate landowner willing to spend the time to entertain them.

But you never can tell if the felling is going to be quick or quiet. During the previous winter, before we set sail for Scotland and were still in Cornwall, anchored close to the river shore, I ferried myself the short distance to the – probably – public beach and snuck into the extensive grounds of an exclusive house set up on the high ground overlooking the confluence of two branches of a river. There stood a huge elm, barkless, long dead, yet still standing because the twists and turns of the river hereabouts – and the fact that it was so well wooded by healthy, leafy trees – took the fight out of gale force winds which might otherwise have blown it to the ground. To reach the tree I had to climb an almost vertical bank to a height of about 50 feet, dragging my chainsaw behind me, sliding back a step for every two I gained. At last I got to the tree, hid among its twisted roots and from there, looked up. At that point I began to have second thoughts. Then thirds. For me to attempt to saw it would be ridiculous – the trunk was too big, for one thing. My saw will cut to a depth of 15in (375mm) – twice that if you saw from both sides. The tree was bigger, prouder, grander than even it appeared to be from the beach, and had a huge span of rotten branches. Not only that, it was much bigger than any tree I had felled before. The final and compelling reason not to fell it was that from up here I could see the mansion to which it belonged, and they could therefore see it. I reasoned with myself for ten minutes, weighing up the pros and cons. There were plenty of cons and the only reason I could think of to take it down was that I didn't like to fail in an endeavour.

What folly pride leads us into. I fired up the chainsaw, and rapidly cut the bird's-mouth – a kind of a wedge-shaped slither of cheese cut from the side of the trunk on which you wish the tree to fall. People who know what they are doing are very accurate with this cut and can fell a tree so that its tip lands on a pile of empty bean-cans stacked for the purpose, as a piece of showmanship, on the ground. I was aiming for the beach. Having made that cut I stopped the saw and sat for another ten minutes filled with regret. Sadly, the tree couldn't be left in that state. I wished to God it could, and I had the leisure to repent a thousand times of ever starting the job. But now that

I'd cut the bird's-mouth the tree was unstable and a danger to anyone walking below. I sat listening to discover whether a gardener or woodsman had heard the noise and was coming to investigate, but the only sound I heard was the beating of my own heart. That's all anyone might have heard who happened to be standing within 50 metres of me.

I never look at the saw when I'm making the final cut, I look instead up into the canopy of the tree – I want to be the first to know when it starts to fall, and in what direction. Then at least I can try to leg it if it looks as though it's going to fall on me. Amongst the upper twigs I saw the first unmistakable signs of movement as they disengaged themselves from the neighbouring trees, and a bit more daylight opened up between them. It was falling the right way. I stopped my saw, put it down on the ground beside me, and sat listening to the popping noises coming from the trunk.

How I wished I hadn't started. The little popping noises soon grew in volume until they were like rifle shot, and multiplied until it sounded as though a whole artillery was letting loose with everything it had in a desperate last stand. Its echo made it sound as though the enemy was returning fire from the opposite bank of the river. When the tree, painfully slowly, began to fall in earnest I saw a large hole opening up in the canopy. It was like one of those films you see about the deforestation of the Amazon. One tree comes down, inadvertently taking the branches of a few others with it, and suddenly there's a hole in the forest the size of a football pitch. When the tree had committed itself to falling and was beyond the point of no return, I discovered that the trunk was hollow, and there began a series of woody explosions, or implosions – or both – shooting powdery debris so far into the sky that it was becoming a nuisance to aircraft. Gradually those bangs joined forces to become a rolling thunder, as though a whole evening's fireworks had inadvertently been set off at once. I muffled the trunk with my jacket to try to cover the noise.

There was a momentary lull whilst the tree was in free-fall down the cliff face – which I had the privilege of enjoying in slow motion – before it hit the beach, apparently setting off land mines down there, so powerful that bits of tree were blown back up to me. Amid all that noise, which will be familiar to anyone used to handling dynamite, it seems unnecessary to say that I felt like an idiot. But sometimes I surprise even myself with my own stupidity. Felling rotten trees is of course extremely foolhardy, and many hapless woodsmen have been killed by a falling branch – *a widow maker* – once the tree begins to move. A professional would limb the tree first.

At last, silence reigned, and a cloud of red dust billowed down the river valley. I followed it with my eye as it rolled into the distance, and wondered if anyone would notice anything unusual.

But back to the present. Here, on the edge of a Scottish forest, dressed in his slippers, standing between two chainsaw hillbillies, was a man who demanded to know what we were doing with his trees. We both looked at Graham.

Graham put on a superior tone, the effect of which was marred by his croaky voice and the fact that the racoon tail of his Davy Crockett hat had somehow managed to work its way round to the front whilst he was sawing, and was now dangling down his face. The casual observer couldn't help noticing that that put its bum on Graham's forehead. It was hard to be proud of Graham just then.

'Erm... I *think* you'll find it's *my* wood,' he croaked, throwing his head back with little jerky movements to try to flick the tail out from his view.

'All this wood belongs to that house,' the slippered man told us, pointing to a house nearby, in case we hadn't spotted it.

'All this wood belongs to the Forestry Commission – apart from the stack on which I'm standing, which belongs to me.' Graham turned the hat sideways, which was a definite improvement and actually looked quite rakish.

What began as a frosty confrontation soon thawed when the stranger told us that he had just bought the place, and that perhaps the mistake was on his side. We got chatting and found that he'd been the skipper of a Baltic Trader owned by Greenpeace – a 'proper' old-fashioned Baltic Trader, timber-built, canvas sails, of which a few examples are still parting the seas a hundred years after they were built. Over a cup of tea he and his South African wife – who was nursing a baby to which she appeared to have given birth only moments earlier – described their life aboard: the privilege of sailing one of these old craft, and the terrifying feeling you got when you looked along its deck in a gale to see it racking over the waves in the manner a caterpillar walks.

We set off back to the yard, newly provided with seasoned larch for firewood – which burns hot:

Flames from larch will shoot up high
Dangerously the sparks will fly.

There are twenty more lines of that Olde English verse yet to recite – I'll try to bring you the rest of it by the end of the book, then you won't be scratching around for things to do during a power cut.

The bowsprit was still broken. We were desperate to get back out to the lochs – away from the sardine crush of other boats, the comings and goings of their owners, and the mechanical clangings of the yard – and were just wondering how to go about it when Steve Thomas phoned. He is my friend who used to spend holidays alone at St Mawes. These days he has a house in Cornwall and was on the blower to ask if we could re-roof a barn belonging to it. Part of the deal was that he'd send us the dosh to buy an old banger so that we could get there. Accommodation would be thrown in.

5 MY EARLY CAREER AS A GREAT YACHTSMAN

PEOPLE CAN BE SUCH FOOLS when buying a second-hand car. They imagine that owning a luxury brand will elevate their status in the world and give them a sort of 'pride of ownership' – attracting to themselves envious glances simply by exhibiting a posh car on their driveway. Second-hand car salesmen are aware of this and double or treble the price an 'exclusive' make of vehicle is actually worth as a mechanical device, then they lie in wait. They snared us. Even apprehending the danger wasn't enough to save Linda and me from falling into exactly the same trap as everyone else – we took the final plunge into insanity and paid £500 for a Skoda. You should have seen us slide pompously behind its leatherette steering wheel, and glide down the salesman's forecourt, piss-wind with importance. Talk about the Emperor's New Clothes.

The Skoda comes with lots of 'toys' – everywhere we looked, levers and switches poked out at us offering to enhance our motoring pleasure: there were four gears (and another one for making it go backwards); a steering wheel (which was a boon, we discovered, for going round corners) and three foot pedals. I pressed my foot down on one of these pedals, and within about a minute Linda and I found ourselves looking first at one another, then at the road ahead, both having formed the distinct impression that we were speeding up; when I floored the pedal next to it, it wasn't long before we formed an equally strong conviction that we were slowing down. The third pedal didn't do anything that we could discover and may have been a spare.

Living on a sailing boat – having that as our main conveyance, and the wind for propulsion – we'd become accustomed to a slower pace of life. At the same time as voyaging we can read a book, go fishing, cook a meal, bake a loaf, or do all of those things at once. But as soon as we pulled out onto a motorway for the first time in years it was apparent that the world had changed. People drive like idiots these days; we were haring along at 40, and they came *flying* past us!

Two exhausting days later we arrived at our destination – Bude in Cornwall – and by the time we parked up, the needle on the petrol gauge showed that half a tank of fuel had been consumed. It may have been faulty – we'd put a tenner's-worth in before we left, and there's no way we could have used all that.

Our bowsprit is curved for the simple reason that the designer thought it would look better that way. He was right, of course. To bend the original – the broken one – we'd sawn a spruce tree in three, lengthways, applied glue to all meeting-faces, supported the ends over a gulley, and then hung a cement mixer from the middle until the glue set. It wasn't very technical but the result was excellent. Its replacement was to be made of cedar, which smells lovely but is also very strong. Durable, too – cedar shingles (wooden slates) are used on roofs, untreated, and last for forty years.

We arrived back at our old boatbuilding barn, which we hadn't seen for four years, and lots of emotions thrilled in our breast. With the single exception of the years we'd spent living on board, the three years we'd spent building our boat – starting with the trees – were the best years of our lives. Our tools were still there, just as we had left them. I'd expected to find that they'd been stolen, or 'borrowed'. We blew the dust off five planks of cedar, sawed them to width, spread glue along their 16ft (5m) lengths and stacked them into a pile. To get the curve, we turned the pile over onto its side, pinned the two ends so they couldn't move, and then pushed the middle away until it 'looked right'. We used a glue called a Resorcinol

Formaldehyde; it's the same stuff they use to make plywood – if you get too close to the tub it comes in, it chokes you, makes your eyes water, and melts the hairs in your nostrils. It's probably terrible for your health – but it is *really* strong glue.

Every foot along the bowsprit's length we clamped it tightly until the glue began to weep from the joins – that way we knew there were no air-gaps. Two days later, when the glue had 'gone off', we started to plane and sand the bowsprit to shape – round at one end whilst leaving it square at the other (to suit the metal fittings on board). When the subtle transition between 'square' and 'round' had been achieved, and we stood back to admire our handiwork, I had no hesitation in offering Linda a 30-year guarantee on it. Varnishing could wait until we'd got it back to Scotland – that way, if it picked up any knocks or marks whilst sliding about on the roof of the Skoda all the way between here and Scotland I could 'sand' them off.

Incidentally, getting ahead of myself, whilst I was applying one of its eight coats of varnish back at Ardfern in Scotland, Princess Anne walked past. *The* Princess Anne. Has she ever done that to you when *you're* varnishing? We didn't speak. I don't think she realised who I was until she'd passed.

Steve's house was a country bank years ago and the outbuilding he wanted me to re-roof used to be a cart-house and stable. The cobbled floor of the cart-house was noticeably furrowed by the wheels of the cart, coming and going. It reminded me of the inside lane of the motorway we'd been stuck on for two days. There was an upper floor to the building – accommodation for the ostler, and next to that a hayloft. The hayloft must have been used to store correspondence at some time because when I was taking the roof off I found an old letter under the eaves, buried by half an inch of dust. Dated during the winter of 1886, it was beautifully written in that impeccable copper-plate hand which was thrashed into every Victorian school child with a whip, its author a farmer, pleading with the bank to arrive at a decision on a mortgage for which he was applying so that he could buy a larger farm. The urgency, he explained, was that he would need to either seed the farm he was on or seed the one he hoped to buy, otherwise he'd lose a year's income.

Later on, when I was dismantling one or two of the roof timbers, I found a rafter which had been signed by a tradesman and dated in the 1860s. *A hundred and forty years* his workmanship had lasted. Something to be proud of. So I wrote his name on the timber I used to replace it, and then underneath I wrote my own name to exonerate him from the inferiority of the alterations.

There was a bit of a coincidence whilst we were in Cornwall. When I was in my twenties I used to sail a lot with a friend of mine called Spearsy, but hadn't seen him for donkey's years. He phoned whilst I was working on the roof and we discovered that, just then, he happened to be in Cornwall too. Back in the 80s he looked like that member of the Village People (who had the 1978 smash hit with their recording of *YMCA*) who wore biking leathers, chains and had one of those drop-handlebar moustaches. You couldn't tell the two apart, actually, and whereas everyone I knew had a poster of Glenn Hughes on their bedroom wall, Glenn had a picture of Spearsy. When Spearsy walked over that Cornish threshold twenty years later I was astonished to see what time had done to him – he was shiny bald and yet had retained surprisingly black eyebrows; it was like he had a couple of offcuts of faux-fur stuck to his forehead. I don't know if he was using some kind of treatment on them. What hadn't changed, though, was that he was still word-perfect with the song, and remembered all the moves.

The first boat I ever owned, and on which Spearsy used to accompany me, was a Westerly GK 29 called *Good Knews*. I think it's in Ireland now. The GK 29 had a reputation for being fast but the price you paid was that they were very light and tender and whenever you stepped on board, the mast would swing toward you and give you a black eye.

My GK 29 was a bit of an impulse buy. In my twenties all I knew about boats was that they were meant to float but sometimes sunk, famously, and with the loss of many lives. What gave me the idea to buy one was that I was working in London and one Sunday in January, without the least interest in botany, decided to visit Kew Gardens. I didn't have any friends so went alone. I was walking with my hands clasped behind my back in the manner that I'd seen other lone visitors walk – it made them look very knowledgeable about plants. I didn't realise back in those days that walking with your hands clasped behind your back, and knowing a lot about plants, are both sure-fire ways of ensuring you never get any friends. Of a sudden the low-hanging fronds of a palm tree brushed through my hair, sprinkling me in a kind of exotic stardust which asked me why I lived as I did?

'Take stock of your life,' it seemed to say. 'Not only are you miserable but you are the cause of misery in others. Why waste yourself in city-work when you could buy a boat, sail to the other side of the world and spend the rest of your life loafing around on white-sand beaches, eating coconuts and bananas?'

The question of whether a GK 29 was a suitable boat to get me there not only never crossed my mind but would have seemed technically irrelevant if it had. In my judgement a boat either floated and was therefore seaworthy, or it had ceased to float and was unsuited to my purpose.

From among the thousands of boats on the market my decision about whether or not to buy *this* boat was strongly influenced by three factors:

Firstly, the bloke who owned it seemed a nice chap – he was a doctor, you know?

Secondly, it was afloat. There could be no doubt about that because when I stuck my arm into the water alongside it I couldn't feel the bottom.

But the clincher – and I wasn't expecting this – was that it had pink racing tape running down either side of the deck.

I was a young man in my twenties and although I was interested in boats, to a degree, I was *more* interested in girls. Instinct told me that those flashy racing strips would be a girl-magnet. In fact, I remember feeling slightly embarrassed that a married man in his forties – and a doctor, at that – could be so *obvious*. There he was standing on deck explaining the advantages of a tri-radial spinnaker when all I wanted to know was how often he'd had to kneel on a Sunday in order to confess another pink-tape triumph. But I couldn't ask him, what with his son standing there. So I bought the boat on trust and hoped that the tape would do its work.

It was only after dinner one evening when I settled down to carry out my intensive planning for a voyage to the other side of the world that it occurred to me it might be nice to go with someone, for company. I imagined that it could take several hours to cross an ocean and it would be nice to have someone to talk to. In many ways my friend Spearsy seemed like the ideal partner: he knew less about sailing than I did, so was unlikely to question my authority, and I like people who laugh easily. Another point in his favour was that Spearsy never *stopped* laughing. The braying of a horse was a whisper to it. God, I can hear him laughing now.

I recognised that the first qualification of a sailing companion was that he – or she – should be of sound mind and judgement, but realised that Spearsy was probably all I could get. We'd worked together for the previous eight months and he'd seemed the happiest man alive, but one day he came into work and a single glance at him told me that his blue skies had turned to grey again – the woman he loved had spurned him. That tragedy launched him into a parallel universe and only his corpse was left dragging itself long-faced through this one. I knew that if I acted quickly I could capitalise on this brief window of grief.

We both worked selling telecoms equipment – he wasn't a successful salesman so I waited for his monthly sales figures to come in and then seized my opportunity to announce the idea of an *around-the-world* adventure at the very moment I knew he would be considering his future.

It's dangerous to embark on a long voyage without the necessary experience so we agreed that in the first instance we'd drift about in the Solent pulling on bits of rope to find out what they did in a variety of conditions not exceeding Beaufort Force 4. Then when we'd got the hang of it, we'd ask someone in which direction we should head off if we wanted to see the Marquesas.

It's strange, but looking back I now see that it is to that period, and to those voyages, that I owe my vast experience as a yachtsman, because whenever we ran aground or sunk a fishing boat and rescued its crew, I was at the tiller and Spearsy was down below making tea. Consequently it was *me* who saw what happened and all the fruits of experience therefore *fell* to me. Spearsy would merely hear a bang, look through the window just in time to see our mast collapsing onto the wreckage of whatever we'd hit, leap on deck, laughing like a drain, and begin hauling people from the water.

Having completed our final preparations we pointed the bow west, and began the voyage which had been almost a month in planning. Miles passed under our keel as we sat contentedly on deck exploring the arts, science, pure mathematics, and the principles of gentlemanly deportment in conversation. Day turned to night, and night to day again when I put up the binoculars and saw that the white sands of the shore to which we were perilously close were backed by palm trees. In the dazzling sun we turned toward it, threw out the anchor as soon as we felt the keel bump, furled our tired sails, and rowed ashore to find ourselves in Torquay.

Spearsy

Before Linda and I could head back up to Scotland we were detained by one further event. During our boat-build in Devon four years earlier we used our old Land Rover to fetch and carry – it had become more than an old friend, it was one of the family, and selling it, now its work was done, was out of the question. Not that you could have sold it. There wasn't a panel on it that wasn't bent, hanging off, or mainly body-filler. One of the last things we did before beginning our new life on board was to drive it to its new home, a farm owned by some friends of ours who had offered us free parking in one of their fields. It had lain there for four years when the dreadful realisation came that we would have to scrap it. The scrap dealer was eight miles away. Would the wheels still turn?

Steve owned a brand-new Land Rover and offered to tow it. The admiration I felt for my mothballed vehicle when Steve was able to pull me out of the muddy field without the slightest hesitation was short-lived. I don't know how much towing Steve has done but driving at almost 50mph along Devon's winding lanes when I had already explained to him that my vehicle had no brakes, and that there would be no servo-assistance on the steering wheel, is reprehensible behaviour. I knew that he wasn't doing it for 'sport' – he just doesn't think sometimes.

We breezed along country roads which although new to Steve were familiar to me and when I realised that in about half-a-mile we would be plummeting steeply downhill, I began to signal him to slow down. I waved to him through the windscreen in that unflappable, restrained sort of manner that Englishmen exhibit just before a crisis, but on we went. I flashed him with my lights, but the battery was dead. I hooted him with my hooter, but not a peep came out of it. I yelled. He didn't hear. I shook my fist at him. He didn't see. And then I waved my arms about like a drowning man, pleading him to stop. As we crested the hilltop I swallowed hard and watched as his vehicle sank from my view. A moment later I was airborne, and followed him in weightless descent. I tried to select a low gear, but the clutch was inoperative and the gear stick only bent when I tried to engage it. I jammed my brake pedal to the floor – heard the metallic clack as it bottomed out in the foot well – but nothing happened. Not only was there no braking effect, it was as though the vehicle had been rifled for spares and the pedal had been disconnected from everything under the bonnet. I screamed.

'STEVE!!!'

But I only saw the lumpish outline of his head, snugged down onto his thick shoulders, staring lamely ahead.

Next I tried the handbrake. It had an almost imperceptibly slight retarding effect on the vehicle. At first waves of joy passed over me, but after it had been pegging us back for about ten seconds, plumes of smoke began rising from the floor of the cab. After another ten seconds I could scarcely see out and to save the vehicle from bursting into flames, let the handbrake off again.

With one white-knuckled hand strangling the steering wheel, and the other waving maniacally out of the window, I flew downhill, scarcely touching the road. I remember how the healthy smells of newly-manured fields blew a steady gale through all the holes in the bodywork, clearing the cab of smoke. Then, a miracle – quite suddenly, having seen my frantic waves of distress, Steve slammed on his brakes. I never saw a vehicle come so quickly to rest. I saw the red-brilliance of his brake lights, noticed his vehicle sink on its suspension – as cars do when braking heavily to avoid an accident, mindless of what's going on behind them – and watched him pull in to the side of the road. All three things happened in but a moment. I said my prayers, knowing that there was nothing I could do, and in the few moments left to me, wondered what Steve's Land Rover would look like when it was about two feet shorter.

I still don't know how this happened, but as his vehicle came to rest at the side of the road, a track appeared on the left – not even a track really, just a short muddy access climbing steeply to a field gate. The start of the track and his brake lights were directly in line, so I jerked my steering wheel to the left, still doing about 50, and shot up the access track, coming to rest an inch from the gate. From where I sat I could look down on Steve's roof. He got out, and we had a bit of a chat.

I don't know if Steve has ever been towed at 50mph in a vehicle with no brakes, and therefore couldn't see things from my point of view, but there were two further incidents during which death or injury were only avoided by the intervention of Jesus Christ. Finally I called a halt to the project a mile from the scrap dealer. The reason was that we were now in a town, about to go down another steep hill, there was a speed limit which I couldn't guarantee to stick to, and mothers pushed children in prams along the pavement on either hand in the belief that it was safe for them to do so. Risking our own lives was one thing – risking someone else's was quite another. Then Steve made a suggestion for which I will always admire him.

'Why don't I reverse up behind you,' he said, 'tie the cars together with you in front, and I'll *lower* you down the hill?'

Genius. Pure genius.

I'll never forget the expressions on the faces of pedestrians as they watched a heaped-up old wreck of a Land Rover with its panels hanging off, towing a showroom-condition Land Rover down a hill.

6 STAGS IN THE GARDEN

WE DROVE THE 700 MILES BACK UP TO SCOTLAND with the bowsprit on the roof, sticking out over both bumpers. At service stations fellow motorists wandered over to our car carrying a cardboard cup of coffee in one hand and half a Cajun chicken wrap in the other. They would chew thoughtfully for a moment, then ask: 'Woss that then?'

'It's a bowsprit for an old-fashioned sort of boat.'

Then they'd nod as though they *thought* that's what it was.

'Where you going?'

'Scotland.'

'Thass a long way, that is.'

It was February, and if Spring hadn't actually sprung we had the feeling that it was about to. Passers-by wore cheerful smiles of hope, the days were growing longer, and the air wasn't as cold as it had been. When I dropped a wrench on deck, mounting the new bowsprit, it didn't ring out clear and cold, as other calamities had during the winter, but fell with a warm thud. Our new bowsprit returned us our freedom.

'I see there's a plot of land for sale on the Isle of Jura... looks nice.'

Linda was flicking through the property pages of the *Oban Times*.

'How much?'

'£40,000. There are two plots, actually.' She showed me the picture – grazing land sloping lazily down to the sea.

'With planning permission?'

'Yup – outline planning permission.'

'What are we doing sitting here?'

It's the great British pastime – browsing estate agents' windows and the property pages. We always look for building plots or mouldering ruins which just happen to have some waterfront where we could moor our boat. Not much comes up.

We sailed out of the marina on a startlingly sunny morning which followed a clear-sky night, a soft wind from the north-west filled our sails, tinkling us over the rippled water in the loch, past the protected eastern side of Eilean Mhic Chrion, with its little patches of white frost nestling amongst clumps of autumn-brown fern, and out into a deserted sea. Nothing moved but us, sailing through a picture postcard.

The pilot's warnings about the Dorus Mor seem to be exaggerated on a morning like this. Our boat heaved once or twice, unexpectedly, as we passed through. The place is littered with rocks and skerries and the tidal stream seemed intent on pushing us onto one of them, but changed its mind at the last minute and returned us to the main stream. Our head swung off suddenly to port, and then to starboard. After that we were through.

We always have misgivings about arriving somewhere which *isn't* a harbour. You need more information than the chart is able to provide – it hadn't been expecting anyone to make a landfall just there and scrimped on the detail for that bit. Jura's east coast is long, straight and hilly. One mile of it is identical to the next and we began to doubt which bit of it we should point the bow at. We got a taste – just a taste – of what it must have been like for Columbus, Cook and Magellan on their voyages of discovery carrying either no chart at all, or else one of those risible scrolls of cloth daubed with almost meaningless lines representing countries their draughtsmen had either never visited or else had made up entirely.

A lot of shipping has been lost refining charts – finding out the hard way where the rocks are. Some of those lost craft have become a nuisance in themselves. As we struck off the well-beaten track on an unlikely course to the shore we were afraid we'd either find one of them, or *become* one of them.

We have a 'routine' for discovering virgin coast. We've honed it and polished it because it works so well. As we approach the shore Linda stands on the foredeck staring into the black depths of the sea, looking out for rocks. She half turns to me and shouts, 'How deep is it here?' only to get much the same answer as she did ten seconds earlier.

The silence is broken again: 'ROCKS!' she yells.

At which I wrench the tiller first to the left then right, accidentally speed up, then throw the engine growling in reverse, whilst leaping about, craning my neck to see the danger I should avoid.

'Oh no... it's all right,' she murmurs, half to herself, unaware of the effect she is having. 'It's only a bit of weed.'

Suddenly she booms out as unexpectedly as a cannon whose fuse no one can remember lighting: 'STOP! I CAN SEE THE BOTTOM!!! I can see the bottom! What's the depth?'

'Sixty metres.'

'Oh? Must be another bit of weed. Yes, don't worry – that's what it is... more weed, Alfie.' With that she half-turns toward me wearing a warm smile, sharing the humour of the situation, and letting me know what a lovely time she's having.

It's a matter of pride in the Navy that no one calls above his speaking voice – that's what lends the ship such a well ordered, mannerly air as she steams unflappably into port. I'd love to have a similar working practice on board our little vessel but Linda comes from a long line of Glaswegian costermongers – folks whose large and powerful lungs remain the inexpensive alternative to Glasgow's local telephone network.

Another slight discrepancy between naval methods and our own concerns insubordination – whereas 'By the mark, fifteen fathoms on sand, sir' is traditional, Linda prefers: 'Hang on a minute – sixty metres? Are you sure you're reading that thing right... only, you know what you're like...'

As we approached we noticed that the shoreline ahead had a bit of a nibble taken out of it, which corresponded encouragingly with the chart, plus a ridge of rock acting like the protective arm of a breakwater ran out to sea. That, too, tallied – this was either a remarkable coincidence or we had come to the right place. We turned into the smooth water behind the arm.

'OK – this'll do... Alfie, drop the anchor down here,' Linda yelled with authority, when we were still a quarter-mile out to sea. We – I, then – like to anchor in the shallowest water we can get away with – 5 metres or even 3 – it's me that has to heave the anchor back up again when we leave, by hand, and dragging up 50 metres of chain because we've anchored in 12 metres of water a quarter of a mile offshore would put me in my box.

When our keel was hovering a few inches above the sandy bottom we rounded up into the chilly breeze, waited for the wind to bring us to a halt, sails fluttering, dropped our anchor – watching it thump onto the seabed and throw up a little cloud of sand, which fell again in slow motion like a snow globe – and pulled the sails down. The breeze blew us back on our anchor, we paid out a miserly 20 metres of chain in a straight line and felt it snub as it came taut. And with that we knew our little ship would still be here when we got home.

Walking up the pristine sand beach with nary a footprint upon it toward a hamlet of stone-built houses, our senses zinged to be making an unannounced arrival on strange soil. Everything we saw took on greater significance than it would normally be allowed, so that when we saw wild red deer grazing in the garden of the first house we came to we rifled through all our previous experience to know whether this *seemed* odd, or actually *was* odd. The deer looked at us with mild interest as we walked by, working their lower mandibles busily. A few moments was all they could spare us, then as if by a signal their heads went down to continue browsing.

The road ahead was a strip of tarmac with no markings, and no edges, laid directly onto the grass in a narrow valley of green. There were five houses in all, yet not a peep, nor puff of smoke, came from any of them. In a few short steps we left the hamlet behind and followed the road, wondering where it would take us. A minute more around a bend a lonely graveyard came into view. No church, just a drystone wall enclosing forty or so gravestones – one of which marked the last resting place of Mary McCraine, died 1856 at the age of 128.

We became aware that the road was taking us the wrong way, or at least the *long* way, and that the building plots we were looking for were not in this valley but in a parallel valley over a hill thickly covered by scrub oak on our left. There were no paths so we struck off toward the trees and immediately found ourselves in a bog. Fortunately it hadn't rained much in recent weeks so we stopped sinking before it reached our necks, climbed out the other side, and then began to claw our way up a steep hill through oak and birch, whose tangling branches swept low over the ground searching for light, making the most of the protection afforded them by the lee of the hill. A hundred metres further up, at the summit, the hilltop was as bald as a mushroom.

Even folk who have never visited a Scottish island have little trouble in imagining that the wind in the Hebrides can be fierce. An islander told us once, as he stood in his garden one ragged morning after a storm, that he had recorded a gust of 107mph.

'See ma shed, there?' he said, pointing a bony finger at a potting shed which lay on its side in his back garden. 'That used to be in ma *front* garden.'

On the hilltop nothing grew taller than heather. As we broke cover we startled a herd of 20 or 30 red deer. In complete contrast to the first herd they no sooner clapped eyes on us than bolted. We watched them stampede down the hill, out of view, and then crest a hill half a mile away, where they stopped and turned to look back. Catching sight of us once more they bolted again to a second hill a mile beyond, and when they bolted from that they disappeared completely. We walked now over ground which human feet seldom trod, and found an antler lying on the ground. It was surprisingly heavy but we carried it in case we should have need of some Stone Age tools.

The next valley was shared by just three houses standing independently of each other, set at a discrete distance, each at a different angle from its neighbour, built in a different style. And in none of them, so far as we could tell, was anyone at home. Although only a few hundred metres from the first, this valley and its beach made an unhappy contrast with the sandy paradise of the one in which we had anchored. Its beach was littered with the blues and yellows of plastic flotsam blown ashore with rotting weed. The grass was a carpet of squeaking, creaking fragments, of half-buried bottles and bits of rubber, and of fishing crates and empty drums of oil, all held in place by grassy roots which had colonised the hinterland between boggy hill and rocky shore, and which formed a course-weave over the sandy soil. Sticking out from black rocks were planks of splintered wood and aluminium fishing floats with tangles of polypropylene rope and nets.

On the plot we had come to see stood the ruin of an old crofter's cottage – a But and Ben with a rusting tin roof, consisting of just two rooms; the one you walked into, and an inner room to the right: one for living, and one for sleeping. Set in the chimney-wall of the living room was a black-iron range with clumpy attachments spreading out from a central fire grate like a prim Victorian fireplace, except that it was suspended a foot or two above the ground. There was a kettle hob, a bread oven to one side, a clothes-iron to the other, and a gridiron through which the flames of a newly-stoked fire could leap, for broiling. The size of the room allowed for just a table and a chair or two besides, and across from that, on which to spend the long winter hours between 'tea' and 'bed' in repose, an easy chair with a candle-holder set in the wall to one side – the better to knit, darn and sew.

Outside, leaning against the building was a timber frame clad in corrugated iron sheets for storing 'peats', and across the ways, hidden deep in the dry brown stems of last year's fern, the remains of a veteran car, an Austin A40, with its metal steering wheel on a spindly column, a few bits of leather and some springs where the painfully narrow seats used to be – separated by a handbrake, which was pulled 'on' – and in each corner of the wreck, showing just above the ground, the arch of four bald tyres with their fabric poking through in places, as thin as bicycle tyres, and no longer fitting onto the spoked wheels they once framed.

For generations this site had been home to a 'comfortable' family; now it was silent, waiting for its next residents, but not for us.

Nets and sticks

As we untied our dinghy from a rock and began to carry it down the sand to the water a woman in her fifties came out from the house on whose lawn the deer were grazing when we arrived, and were still grazing now – they didn't stop grazing as she ran past waving her arms. She called after us: 'Hello!'

'Hello...'

'Is that your boat?'

'Yes.'

'Lovely – we don't get many boats in here... How long are you staying?'

'Just off, actually... We came to look at those building plots.'

'What did you think?'

'Well, if they'd been in *this* bay... but *that* bay is a bit... you know, *lovely* – but a bit, sort of...'

'Yes... I know.'

Her blonde hair was flicked back carelessly by the wind, adding wildness to her attractions. She spoke in the unhurried way that remote-livers do, unafraid, self-assured, but slightly unreachable. She didn't have an island accent, though her family had lived there for generations. She'd moved away to London and to Australia for a while but eventually returned to carefree Jura to bring up her family. Now that her daughter had grown up she too had left home. It's hard to imagine what Jura could offer a young adult, but when you've travelled about a bit it seems to have most of the things you've been searching for.

'Are there any other plots on Jura, perhaps near trees?' we asked.

'No... plots don't come up very often.'

One of the joys of travelling is meeting new people – and one of the costs of always moving on is that those meetings don't become lasting friendships. We walk only reluctantly away from strangers whose company we've enjoyed – people who would become good friends if we were staying. But we're not; we're sailing away.

We hoisted a generous amount of canvas, for the benefit of an old seagull who was sitting on the rocks waiting for a meal. We sailed our anchor out of the ground in the way that old sailors did, gathering in chain hand over hand as the boat moved herself up to the spot where the anchor lay, then tying off the chain and tripping it off the seabed, and filling-away out of harbour as they did in the days before engines had been invented. The old seagull hadn't seen it done that way for a hundred years, and chattered his approval.

The anchor clunked into place on the metal bow roller. The hills echoed back to us in adieu. Our boat's head fell off the wind, and once the rocky shore had slipped astern only the tinkling water from our bow, and the gentle nodding of our boat, told us that we were under way. We pointed our nose south, filling the sails to a crisp February breeze, and with the tide doing most of the work, set off for Islay. Linda was down below, beginning preparations for dinner. She popped her head out of the hatch from time to time, holding a vegetable peeler in one hand, unseeing, blinking occasionally, lost in her own thoughts.

7 NORTHBOUND BUS HEADING SOUTH

WE WERE HEADING FOR ONE OF THOSE TINY HARBOURS you get on Hebridean islands which are really just dark pools of water orphaned from the sea by guardian rocks surrounded in foam.

Islay – famed all over the world for making whisky with names you can't pronounce – held a place dear in our hearts as we'd borrowed the name of our vessel *Caol Ila* from one of its distilleries. With a mile to go before we got into the little harbour at Lagavulin, and all the time in the world to complete that mile, we put up the binoculars and spotted the entrance. There was so little wind in our sails that we weren't expecting to arrive for an hour, but wind can be fickle and all of a sudden – as though a fan had been turned on somewhere – it began to blow at Force 7. Now, Force 7 is nothing to write home about... but *this* Force 7 was nearly our undoing.

Because we'd been drifting along in light airs we had a *lot* of sail hoisted high up the mast – too much for a near-gale. Our first indication that something was wrong came when our boat was thrown flat over onto its side with half the deck awash. It wasn't so easy to steer like that and we started barrelling along at breakneck speed through rocks and shoals which demanded to be taken slowly, savoured, admired – but most particularly avoided. What we'd normally do in those conditions, when we were pressed too hard by the wind – and the text books would nod approvingly of this – is to 'round up', as sailors call it: allow the boat to steer itself round until she's pointing her nose directly *into* the wind, comes to a stand-still, sails fluttering like sheets on the line and gives you a chance to unpeg some of it. But in the present circumstance we couldn't alter course because we had rocks on either side obliging us to carry on sailing toward the tiny harbour entrance with the wind coming from the direction which makes boats sail at their most heroic speeds – namely the 'quarter', by which is meant 'behind you, and off to one side'.

Just then a worrying noise started up. It was coming from underwater – an urgent banging, as though someone was trying to get in. Linda and I frowned at one another and wondered who it could be. We hadn't heard the noise before, and in any case weren't expecting visitors, so our minds arrived at the next possibility which was that something was about to fall off, and braced ourselves in readiness for it. We didn't know *what* was going to fall off, and accepted that we would only find out when it did.

Unable to do anything about that for the present, we busied ourselves with other things: we let the mainsail out as far as it would go to try to reduce speed so that instead of catching the wind it fluttered like a flag, or nearly so – not fluttering, but just 'set'. Spilling the wind like that allowed the boat to come upright again, and to our relief normal steering was restored. But for sheer sailing efficiency our boat found that she preferred it and we surged on toward the harbour entrance, carving furrows over the brows of waves as we rose over them and left them behind, hissing with foam in our wake. Had either of us the presence of mind to read the speed log we would have seen something to remember but other thoughts occupied us.

The harbour toward which we were heading wasn't much used by yachts at all, home instead to two or three open boats belonging to fishermen who set pots along these rocky shores, and who could, doubtless, navigate the entrance in their sleep. How we wished one of them was on board with us now to place a guiding hand on our tiller. The entrance was a narrow gut of water 8 metres wide and 3 deep, our course lay between two rocks which rose sentinel above the foam like bad teeth – each marked with a post, one red and one green, to state the bald fact that, incredible though it may seem, here was the entrance. Neither did the entrance form a straight line in and out, but required you to steer a swan-neck course as you passed between them. If you were driving a car through that little chicane, you'd slow down to a crawl – yet we were doing our best speed.

Inside the entrance, the harbour was tiny – sticking with the vehicle analogy for a moment, sailing 15 tons into it at full speed was like driving a lorry into a municipal car park at 70mph (if lorries do 70mph) and it was difficult to imagine how we would stop, avoid carrying away their pier, sinking someone's boat at its moorings, or piling ourselves onto the rocky shore.

Next I tried to get some sail down and began with the biggest foresail, the jib. Ours is stuck precariously out in front of the boat, over the water, secured at the end of our brand-new bowsprit. You don't see many bowsprits these days, by the way, but they were very popular in the 1800s, when life was cheap. However, they're beginning to make a bit of a comeback now that a new invention has made the sacrificing of boys – whose job it was to climb out to the end of them, hell or high water – obsolescent. Today, bringing in the jib is simplicity itself: you pull on a length of rope, conveniently placed within arm's reach of you, which in turn revolves a drum – just like pulling cotton from its reel – and the revolving drum rolls the sail up. Unfortunately, and not for the first time, as I pulled ours it jammed.

The harbour entrance was by this time half a mile away – less than three minutes at our present speed. So I set about the 'other' way of getting a jib down, untying the rope which holds it up the mast, and letting it down on that. Things turn nasty when you take sails down the 'other' way in a squall – ropes begin to crack like a whip around your ears, threatening to have your eye out, or jerk you overboard if it can catch hold of one of your limbs, and the sail-cloth inflates and deflates explosively and with such violence that it looked as though our mast would be torn out of the boat by its roots, taking everything else with it. One moment the mast was bending like an archer's bow, the next it was shuddering like an arrow which had just found its mark.

I let out mile after mile of rope to get the sail down and only knew I'd won when it gave one last half-hearted gasp and collapsed into the sea. Out of spite I left it there to drown for a few moments before heaving it back on board as a fisherman heaves his net.

The excitement of watching Linda and I thrashing about in a crisis, knee-deep in canvas and with bits of rope knotted round our ankles, will be familiar to anyone who has joined us aboard for a quiet sail. But others can simulate the spectacle by unpegging a wedding marquee during the speeches when there's a hurricane blowing outside, and settling back to watch how they deal with it.

By the time the jib was tied securely on deck we had arrived within metres of the harbour entrance and I rushed back to the mast like someone who has one more thing to do before he dies. There I untied a rope – known as a peak halyard – which allows the gaff to droop and the mainsail cloth to hang in folds, thereby reducing its drive. (The gaff, by the way, is that huge piece of timber which is suspended in the air like the jauntily-cocked semaphore arm of a railway signal.) Then I leapt back to rejoin Linda in the cockpit. During the whole performance she'd had been yelling at me, her words whipped away on the wind. Sometimes Linda's yelling conveys interesting information which I am sorry to miss, and sometimes she is merely hurling abuse, which I'm not. Invited to repeat her words now that I was at hand and could hear them, she persuasively expressed a desire *not* to be the one steering the boat when we made our entrance. So I took the tiller from her and we sat wide-eyed to see how fate would play her hand.

The wind, now that it could do us no more harm, dropped down a notch, and at the speed of an ocean racer coming over the line we slipped between the rocks guarding the harbour entrance, splashing them with our wash. I was just thinking what a grand photo it would have made when I saw a flash go off from the end of the pier.

Within yards of the beach we rounded up to wind, canvas shaking, bounced the boats which lay on their moorings with our impressive bow wave, rushed forward to chuck out our anchor – which is always ready for a crisis – settled back on our chain, and as soon as all the canvas had been torn down from its place high above our heads and was lying in untidy heaps around us, the wind fell so light that a feather dropped from the masthead would have drifted down the hatch.

It still amazes me that the mast stayed up. I *built* that mast, and for a month after we launched our boat, whilst we were sorting out the last remaining jobs and still tied to a pontoon where folk could easily get to us – circumnavigators, riggers, soothsayers, premonitors, dockside oafs, and people who were only out doing their shopping – would stop all of a sudden and crane their heads into the air to look up at it.

Then they'd put down their bags, throw a petitioning arm around my shoulders, take me to one side, and through a toothless grin say something like: 'Won't do, will it? It's all wrong... too thin – what's it made of, anyway?'

'Spruce.'

'Spruce!' They'd jump back, wide-eyed with astonishment. 'Spruce, you say? Well, bless you! Spruce... what, like a Christmas tree? Ooh, no, my 'ansome... that won't do at all!'

Having won my attention they'd urge me – if I placed any value at all on my life – not to set out to sea with the mast I'd built – and on no account was I to risk Linda's. They hadn't met Linda yet, but a glimpse of her over my shoulder had ignited a testosterone-fuelled attraction for her. They wanted to protect her and were already dreaming of replacing me (and my mast) and setting off with her – an owl and a pussy cat – to explore the ocean wide. Consequently, at the first sign of any dissent on my part with the plans they proposed, they were quite ready to ditch the friendship they'd struck up with me, and to take up with her instead.

Pretending their warnings didn't sting I returned their generosity by referring them for their improvement to the book by whose authority I'd built a spruce mast: *Gaff Rig* – it's called, and it's by my hero, John Leather.

'John who?'

'He's the world's leading authority on gaff rig...'

'Never heard of him – but if you will have the sense to listen to me I can tell you, standing here, that *that* mast won't work.' Then, having warned me – as their conscience required – they would draw Linda's attention to their chivalry by fixing her with a steady gaze and a baffled expression which was meant to convey the words: *It's no use – I can't seem to get through to him...* Then they'd signal to her with raised eyebrows by way of enquiring whether or not she was ready to ditch me. Happily for me she wasn't, so with an injured air they'd turn their backs on the pair of us, and leave us to our fate, taking up their shopping once more to roll away and perform the Lord's work on less barren ground.

Whenever I had occasion to climb the mast, after that, to its very top – or we were caught at sea in a gale, far from the calming influence of a harbour wall – their kind words would echo back and forth through my mind, and I would wonder if they were right after all. Neither could I help noticing, when I was working at the masthead, that the hollow piece of mast around which my legs were entwined was, in fact, *thinner* than my legs and bending with the strain of keeping a slightly overweight bloke suspended 50 feet above the rolling deck.

Ruined farm

It was primarily to poke about the ruins of a stone-built farmhouse – also for sale at a bargain price – that we had come to Islay, but having trekked, gasping for breath, to the top of the hill on which it stood we realised we'd arrived too late to save it. It had some roughly built outbuildings which formed a sort of west wing which were in much better condition than the main house – being about five hundred years more recent – but they weren't *worth* saving. Inside the house – if you can describe yourself as being inside a house which hasn't had a roof for fifty years – in what would have been the kitchen, the skeletons of two sheep, together with what remained of their wool, were glued to the muddy floor, and lay where they fell against the wall which had offered them protection from the bitter wind during their last infirmity. I climbed a staircase – it must have been a very old staircase because it was made of stone – and up there I could stand precariously on top of what was left of the crumbling wall, two feet thick, and filled with rubble, to take in the view.

The farmhouse stood just as the particulars had described, 'on a hilltop with distant views of the Atlantic' in one direction, and of a young softwood forest in the other – nakedly exposed to all the weather the Atlantic Ocean could throw at it. Today there was a bitingly cold wind – even the grass clung flat along the ground, as though it had been combed. Most days, judging by the soft mud, rain lashed the ruin so hard that even its hilltop elevation wasn't always enough to drain it. The building had about it the atmosphere of unfinished business – as though its thriving, even prosperous, life had ended quite suddenly. Things lay where they had last been used: agricultural equipment half-buried by time with tyre-less wheels, as used in the days of the working horse – an era which ended later here than elsewhere in Britain.

We walked back down the hill. Our feet fell on hard land that hadn't been worked for a generation or more, land that would need stronger arms and more cunning to reclaim it than we could offer. A farmer turned off the road and onto our track, bouncing around as unsecured cargo behind the wheel of his pick-up truck as he negotiated the rain-scoured ruts. We met at the bottom of the hill, where he stopped alongside us and lowered his window. Everyone seemed to have time to chat – perhaps out of politeness, perhaps out of plain-old human nosiness. He poked his head half out of the window.

'It's a grand day!' he called into the wind.

We joined him, leant against his truck and petted a sheepdog in the back who kept his ears pinned flat against his face for warmth. It looked at us, pleadingly. *Please be brief*, it seemed to say.

The farmer's face was carved with what in any other region of the UK would be smile lines – but hereabouts strong wind is such a perpetual feature of the weather that squint-lines are inherited genetically, and babies are born with them. We wondered if he might be the owner of the ruin, and so after the usual British preliminaries, whereby we establish amongst ourselves whether yesterday was colder than today or if it's the other way round – and what the prognosis is for tomorrow – we mentioned that we'd been up to have a look at the farmhouse. There was a stony silence during which his face fell to something approaching pity, and he searched for an encouraging remark, eventually settling for: 'Not much happens up there...' He raised a pair of shaggy eyebrows to throw a glance in its direction and see that he was right. His words seemed to imply a deeper warning.

We stocked up with provisions in the island supermarket, whose shelves I had imagined would be stacked with sacks of weevily flour, candles, and barrels of seal oil – but instead found them neatly arranged with all the goodies you'd expect to find in West Kensington, with the possible exception of Goji berries.

We hitched back to the boat. The generosity of islanders surprises visitors. You walk along the roadside with your thumb out and a vehicle going the other way stops.

'It's a grand day!' they call through the missing window, as the wind blows their hair in several different styles a second. 'I canna stop because I've got to get to Jimmy Campbell's and he shuts at five on a Wednesday. My sister's coming from Glasgow and I'm needin' some eggs to see will I make a quiche...' they explain, '...but I just wanted to say: I hope you get your lift soon! Where are yous headed anyways?'

'Port Ellen.'

'Port Ellen is it?'

'Yes.'

'Och – you'll get a lift there nay bother! Nay bother at all!'

And with that they engage first gear and begin slowly pulling away, waving farewell as they go, veering all over the road, and calling out messages of hope as they bottom-out in a pot hole: 'See you... bye just now – and good luck!'

The next vehicle to pass is a tractor growling along at 8mph. Tractors have only one seat and it would therefore be illegal to carry any passengers. Regardless of that, two people are already standing either side of the driver, arched over him, carrying bags, and with their heads bent against the underside of the roof – they let go of their handholds in order to be able to wave as they pass, and convey the message 'I'm afraid we're a wee bit tight in here as it is!'

There are buses on the island – even the post van doubles as a bus – and we would have caught one if it hadn't shot past us without stopping. It was all a misunderstanding on our side: wanting to head to the south part of the island we mistakenly stood on the side of the road which heads south. But of course what happens is that the bus picks southbound people up from the northbound side of the road, then does a three-point turn and heads south; its driver sailed past us with a supremely confident smile – even waving as he went – as much as to say, 'I know why you're standing there at your southbound bus stop – yous all wantin' to go north, isn't it?'

Asking why the bus does that produces the interesting information that 'that is what it does'.

We got a lift from someone who wasn't going that far – but did anyway. He would have made a fascinating guide to the island if we had understood a word he was saying, but we only managed to pin down about one in twenty, and therefore missed learning 95 per cent of the island's history.

Goods arriving at Bowmore Harbour – fairly recently

We stayed a day or two in the harbour, taking walks along the wild coastline to Caribbean white-sand beaches incongruously littered with sheep dung. Farmyard smells were curiously mingled with those remembered from bucket-and-spade holidays of childhood: saltwater and seaweed. We followed sheep tracks in the sand as they meandered in single file, threading their way through rocks whose crevices sprouted last year's Sea Campion, dehydrated and shivering in the breeze, and on to new grazing, fields of green which intermingled with the sand almost at the high water mark of the beach. Rabbits drummed before shooting into their burrows, and at first sight of us the sheep, unused to humans, scattered over the rocks and bolted for cover like deer, into the stunted oak woodlands which darkly overhung the beach.

At the water's edge the sand was washed continually by turquoise wavelets dashing themselves onto the shore, turning over prettily coloured cowrie-shells, and smudging out the footprints left by a group of sandpipers that teetered along ahead of us. There was something queer about the beach, to use an old-fashioned expression: it was fragile, yet unbroken. A single storm would have desecrated it, had the trees out by their roots, torn chunks from the grassy banks, rucked the sand into heaps and scours, and flooded the fields beyond into salt marsh where nothing grows. But the violence of the stormy waters for which the area is famous was tamed well out to sea by a milky-way of rocks which could be seen scattered like crumbs onto the surface of the water stretching for a mile toward the horizon. Out there stormy seas thrashed themselves to pieces so that even in a hurricane of wind all that remained of towering waves, by the time they reached the shore, were these same little wavelets which lapped at our feet now, toying with the sand.

The protection of the weedy rocks made a haven for seals and otters. We could see them when they surfaced for air. Only the snorkel-noses and half-a-head of the seals showed above water, slowly bobbing up and down like corpses. They'd take noisy breaths, great nervous-sounding sighs of air like prank phone-callers, before sliding back under the water – slow as submarines – where they'd stay for five minutes or more, winding their way through fronds of kelp, hoping to surprise a fish. Otters splashed at the surface, never still for a moment, lawless, sharp, and always on the lookout for some trouble they could cause.

We'd heard an island chronicle that it was on these rocks in the 1700s that a boat foundered in a storm, and the handful of survivors to make it to the shore were taken in, fed and nursed by a small farming settlement, consisting of half a dozen houses. Unbeknown to the sailors and villagers alike, the wrecked ship carried plague, and one by one the sailors died. Then the villagers began to fall ill. They voluntarily quarantined themselves from neighbouring islanders who, when the villagers were too weak to fend for themselves, left food parcels every day in a cleft of rock, nearby. Eventually the food parcels were no longer collected. The islanders waited two weeks, then entered the village to find that the entire settlement had been wiped out by disease. They burnt the houses and bodies where they lay, and the abandoned village has never been occupied since.

Walking inland we noticed, not for the first time, that there were no footpaths, no signs to show you where you might go. It seems strange to me, as someone who grew up in the south east of England – where walkers are herded along paths physically constrained on either side by barbed wire fencing, or morally constrained by notices warning you to *Keep Out* – that in Scotland, a country which has no laws of trespass, where you can walk just about anywhere you please, there are so few 'footpaths'. Is it because when you have the freedom to walk *anywhere* nowhere becomes a beaten track, or is that if you live in an area of wild beauty which you can admire every time you look out of your window, no one walks in it at all?

The way we walked, stumbled really, from our boat along the coast to the beach was the wrong way. I don't know if there is a right way, but the way we went was hard walking; when it wasn't boggy, the ground consisted of huge boulders hidden under dense vegetation, and at every third step we jarred our ankles sliding off them.

We left the islands one morning after breakfast and ablutions. We hoisted a cautious spread of sail and offered it to a cold, dry and steady breeze from the north, hauled up our chain and our anchor hand-over-hand, secured it on deck, pointed the bow toward the harbour entrance, and began drifting slowly, silently, gathering way, eventually reaching the sort of speed at which we would like to have arrived, gently folding back the water with our bow. It's at times like these that it occurs to you that a sailing boat is the ultimate travelling machine. You have only to weigh anchor, set your canvas to the breeze, and the whole world is before you.

Outside the harbour, although there wasn't a cloud in the sky, the sea was a morbid battleship grey, as though it had yet to take off its winter coat and was compelled to be cheerless until April. We passed close by a reef on our way to the southerly point of the off-lying dangers, passing within twenty metres of it to take a closer look. It wasn't always there – like a magician's trick it rose from time to time, throwing water from the flat table of its surface and until that moment giving no clue of its presence. The water on which we sailed was rising and falling so slowly in the long Atlantic swell – like the heaving chest of a giant – that we didn't notice we were being raised and lowered two or three metres, several times a minute. But when the breathing ocean exhaled in a deep sigh, and we sank low in its trough, it was then that the barnacled reef would be revealed, hissing, as water caught by surprise fell back to the sinking sea. Having avoided the danger of splintering ourselves to match-wood on this outlier, we knew that we could set a course which would hug the coast up to the Sound to the north. We rolled peacefully over the sea toward the white speck of a lighthouse low over dark rock, then away up the Sound on the magic carpet of the tide.

Once or twice during the day we distantly saw a coastal fishing boat 'at the prawn', and two Cal-Mac ferries passed one another as they simultaneously worked the outward and return leg of an island service. Apart from that, we were alone.

In the afternoon we gave the Corryvreckan a wide berth. Anyone who owns a boat and thinks of sailing it in Scotland hears – before they hear anything else – about the Corryvreckan. 'One of the most notorious stretches of water anywhere around the British Isles,' says the Yachtsman's Pilot for that area. And since that series of publications has described all 11,000 miles of the British coastline, we feel compelled to sit up and take notice.

It lies between the southern end of the uninhabited island of Scarba and the northern end of the Isle of Jura. Whenever we've passed by it always looks a bit flat so that descriptions we've read of giant whirlpools, and of static waves standing eight metres high, seem to go too far, but I suppose those who have lost their lives to the Corryvreckan may have drowned with the dying thought that they didn't go quite far enough.

The two principal dangers of waves and whirlpools are caused in part by the tidal streams, which are so strong that boats that only intended passing by at a distance can be drawn into its trap. You know how it is when you gently place the nozzle of a Hoover alongside a fly which has fallen asleep on the dining room window and then switch on. As soon as the nozzle begins to suck, the fly – suddenly realising that his life is in danger – takes off, and accelerates smartly away in the direction of safety, his little airframe bouncing gently to eddies in the slipstream caused by your Hoover. But it's too late – although his senses tell him he's doing fifty miles an hour, *you* can see that he is hanging stationary in the air, and beginning to make heavy weather of it. You wait patiently, aware that there's a limit to how long he can keep this up. At last he begins to tire and the distance between him and your nozzle becomes fascinatingly small. You swallow drily, unable to take your eyes off the spectacle. When his back legs – which are swinging about in a relaxed sort of manner – are no more than an inch from nozzle, the fly notices for the first time that there is something behind him, and makes the fatal mistake of looking over his shoulder to see what it is. A moment later there is a *ffwopp* as he disappears down the nozzle, followed by a tapping noise from the inside of the hose – once on each bend – bearing witness to his onward journey. So it is with the Corryvreckan.

George Orwell – who famously wrote his book *Nineteen Eighty Four* near here – only narrowly avoided drowning in the Corryvreckan along with members of his family. They'd taken a rowing boat into the gulf for a pleasure trip but lost control in a series of whirlpools. Their boat was dashed against a rocky island in the heavy swell where it capsized, throwing them all out, but they managed to climb onto the rock and were rescued, not without risk, an hour and a half later by a passing lobster fisherman.

Linda and I once stayed at the house in which Orwell wrote. Barnhill is a two-storey building (not many old island houses are two-storey), damp, gloomy, yet shabbily comfortable as long as both solid-fuel stoves are belching out heat – which is a necessity even in July. There is no mains electricity, although if you turn a light on moments later you hear a generator fire up in an outbuilding; another ten seconds and the light bulb begins to glow vaguely, pulsing with the engine revs. The house has small windows – but windows which, nevertheless, look out on views that cram in more unspoilt panorama per square inch of glass than any window anywhere in the world.

Orwell wrote from a small upstairs room sitting in front of such a window, gazing out over a swathe of green meadow in which deer graze quietly on the gentle slope which falls to the glittering sea, and onwards over five miles of salt water to the mainland, and the ancient emerald green oak forests of Argyll.

By way of emphasising the remoteness of Barnhill, the island road doesn't reach it but gives up four miles short. What takes over from there is the roughest, ankle-jarring track, scraped out over bare rock along which the best transport would be a pack-horse, the worst a 4X4. Barnhill is not lived in, but let by the week to folk who don't mind midges and aren't afraid of isolation. Yet it wasn't always so isolated. The population of many of the Scottish islands has fallen dramatically over the past 200–300 years, and some which were populated are now uninhabited. Between Barnhill and the Corryvreckan there is just one other house which is lived in, permanently, making it one of the remotest continually-inhabited houses in Britain. This solitary house – *Kinuachdrachd* (Kinoctra) – stands where once there was a bustling village, home to twelve families who operated what was in those days the island's main port. Ninety years ago the ferry service ceased; today two people have got almost 20 square miles of island to themselves. Perhaps the Corryvreckan was responsible for the port's downfall – you can't stick to a timetable if your boats don't come back.

8 AN ARGUMENT WITH A STRANGER

THE ISLAND OF LUING, famous for having its own breed of cattle, was a barren-looking place. I wandered over field and moor, losing myself in thought, remonstrating with myself out loud sometimes as I went. I'd been walking up a motorway of a farm-track – deserted, and black with autumn's mud, which was rutted from the passing and re-passing of heavy vehicles. It wound its way silently up a hill toward an enormous but solitary farm shed which I could see for five minutes or more before I got to it blowing steam at every breath. I've noticed in the country that if you wish to remain unseen in the open you should lean, motionless, against a large building. So it was with the farm shed. Only when I had virtually arrived at it did I notice that leaning against it, watching my approach, was a young woman with raven black hair falling about her shoulders who, having stepped out of a Jane Austen novel, stood staring levelly at me with dark eyes, beguiling beauty and unshakeable confidence. I was confused and unmanned by the sight of her and wondered how much of my raving madness she'd seen or heard. I babbled out a shy greeting and walked on. A sweetly-tuned reply followed me.

There is a lady sweet and kind, was never face so pleased my mind, I did but see her passing by, and yet I love her til I die – Thomas Forde (attr) (1580–1648)

You could live amongst the islands in the waters around Loch Melfort for a whole year without tiring of the scenery, the prehistoric interest of the land which surrounds you, or ever needing to move on because of a hurricane.

I dropped Linda off at an abandoned and rickety old wooden pier in Asknish Bay mindful of the fact that if I touched it, it might collapse. I lay our port side against one of its groynes as though our boat were a baby, and the pier its crib, but Linda refused to jump.

'Half the boards are missing!' she said.

'You'll be all right.'

'No – it doesn't look safe.'

'It'll take *your* weight – and in any case, I can't keep the boat here long.'

Only the strong allure of a shopping trip in Oban compelled her to try it with her weight, and as I reversed back out into deeper water I could scarcely take my eyes off my angel: dressed, coiffured and made-up to perfection, picking her way along the rotting and abandoned pier which led to the nameless stretch of road which would take her into 'town'. When she reached the safety of the shore, she turned and waved triumphantly before setting off, her feet lightly tripping up the beach.

Linda and I get on like a house on fire – which is useful when you spend months on end in each other's company. But that doesn't mean we never fall out. Once or twice a year an argument will break out, we have a yelling match for a few minutes – and then a pound to a penny it'll be followed by three days of silence. In the first white-heat of the disagreement one or other of us will row away in the dinghy – deliberately marooning the other – and take a *really* long walk ashore. It's strange how you can go three days in a tiny environment like a boat without speaking to the person with whom you share the space – mealtimes, bed and bath – but somehow we manage it. Our arguments are always about silly things – and in any case we can never remember *what* they were about when they're over. We've learned that it pays to do things separately sometimes, spend a day apart.

Andy phoned. He was a joiner friend of ours who had built the cockpit for the boat, the cockpit in which I now stood.

But we'd known him for way longer than that. For years if ever we were walking along the High Street of a Devon town and spotted through the crowds a well-muscled, bare-chested young man walking toward us on a freezing cold morning in January, we knew that we were about to enjoy an hour in the company of our old friend Andy.

Whilst boatbuilding, he'd worked alongside us for a month or two doing the clever bits of fitting-out the accommodation with an undeflatable cheerfulness. At 8am he'd look forward to Elevenses; at 11 he'd look forward to lunch; at lunch, tea; and at tea, dinner – yet there wasn't an ounce of fat on him even though he celebrated all those occasions by throwing open the lid of a box which you expected to be filled with tools, but which turned out to be a hamper. Andy had served a joinery apprenticeship, and there aren't many of them to be had. He worked quickly and accurately, and cried real tears of joy whenever I broke the tail off one of my doves, or snarled up the best face of a piece of timber with an out-of-control power tool.

He'd phoned to say that he'd just bought himself a boat – a Picarooner, built by the much lamented Martin Heard – and was wondering if I could teach him to sail it when we returned to Cornwall. Nothing would bring me more pleasure. It left me with a warm glow to chat and laugh with Andy on a chill February day. And how much better to chat to him on the phone than meet him in the pub – a man who wears few clothes has no means of carrying a wallet.

The following morning Linda and I headed out, sailing south on a bright blustery day, with our sails deep-reefed. The sea around the islands at the Southern end of the Firth of Lorn is always confused – the tide breaks off at odd angles to pass obstructions, then rejoins the flow from an entirely new direction with the result that the sea was humped-up here, and collapsing there, like boiling treacle. Over all this confusion we leapt and scudded, heeled to the breeze, surging along in a lively manner that makes it good to be alive, and with a refreshing couple of buckets of seawater being thrown onto our backs every minute.

A lively sea

Arriving from the north, the entrance to Loch Craignish lay on the far side of the hazard known as the Dorus Mor. In a hierarchy of nautical infamies it doesn't occupy the very top rungs and we hadn't had a bad experience of it on any of the previous occasions we'd passed through, but now that we had the wind blowing in one direction and a spring tide in the other, it took us quite by surprise. The atmosphere on board was relaxed, and we were winding down in the belief that we were nearly at the close of our day's sail – so we had a double-take when we came around the corner and found ourselves confronted by waves at head-height breaking in all directions. Moments later they were smashing themselves against the hull, or opening up great chasms close alongside, into which our vessel tripped and fell. On one hand lay the black shores of Craignish Point; on the other, its off-lying island. Between the two we ran the seething gauntlet. The air was filled with a restless roar as onto those shores, so close by, these aimlessly unpredictable hummocks of water collapsed, ending their lives in foam.

The maelstrom was interspersed with smooth-looking patches – and our first plan was to steer for those – but just as we reached them they too reared up like giant bubbles in a cauldron. Next we thought of turning back to go the long way round, but now found that once we were in it, steering had little or no effect. Eddies in the water spun us first in this direction, then in another, and all we could really do was to hold on to something and hope that the ordeal didn't last for very long.

Halfway through the ride we noticed that the rocky shoreline which used to be 200 metres away on our left was only 30 metres away and we were heading for it. I looked at the depth sounder to see how long we'd got before we were on the rocks – it was 8 metres (25ft) and falling. I threw the tiller over and began adjusting the sails to suit only to find, the next time I looked up, that we were well off the shore – a counter current having already carried us out close to the island – and my adjustments were helping it along. We gybed again.

Whenever we gybe two or three times in quick succession, we struggle to keep up with the paperwork. Yards of rope lie in tangles around our ankles, like spaghetti, on the cockpit floor. Our arms work like spinning machines, pulling bits of rope from under each other's feet, coiling it and then handing it to the other person in the belief that it belongs to their side of the boat, and they'd better have it. Meanwhile our boat crabbed across the current toward the mainland once more. When Linda next looked up she'd lost her bearings – at the best of times she doesn't like it when the boat points in one direction but travels another – so she let out one of her screams, just to let me know how she was feeling about life. A minute later the sound of tumbling water was behind us and we arrived onto the flat, sluggish water near the entrance to the loch, blinking, and wondering what all the fuss had been about.

Next time we go through the Dorus Mor we'll keep our engine running, or better still, get out on Craignish Point and walk round to meet our boat at the other end, if she's still afloat.

Graham went through the Dorus Mor on his way to Hawaii. I'm getting ahead of myself here because he didn't go through until later that summer – but I might not get the chance to mention it in its proper place. He went to sea with a dozen or so of my nautical publications and I haven't got them back yet. If this tired old world is to have anything from me in return for all the food I've eaten, and all the air I've breathed, let it be this: never lend anyone a book. Not even this one.

From my copy of *Hydrographic Office: Directions for Sailing Vessels 'Going Foreign'*, Graham learned that the general idea for vessels leaving the UK was to get into a position off the south western tip of Ireland, head south until the butter melts, then steer west. Later editions were forced to revise that advice: what with butter being imported from all over the world nowadays, quality varies, and butter melts at different temperatures with the result that some vessels were turning west too soon, whilst others never did turn west. The rules are more relaxed now – most vessels sail south to the Canary Isles on account of its lively club-scene and only head west when they've been refused further credit at the bar.

Furthermore, Graham learned that although it's 7,000 miles from Scotland to Hawaii 'as the crow flies', boat owners are compelled to go where there is water, and *sailing* boat owners are further inconvenienced by the requirement to follow ocean currents and trade wind routes, so that by the time you've read the small print you're looking at a voyage of 12,000 miles. Nevertheless, even long journeys begin with a first step and a voyage to Hawaii from Ardfern, Scotland, begins by sailing through the Dorus Mor.

Graham had shipped a friend along to teach him the ropes and having decided to take a laid-back approach to the actual time of departure from the marina they arrived at the Dorus Mor – four miles away – after dark, and when it was at its most lively. Their first apprehension of danger came from the sound of crashing water which, not surprisingly, they found unnerving – the more so because they couldn't see where it was coming from. Shortly Graham's boat bounced and span in circles – much as ours had – as they were dragged into the turbulent waters in the gap between the unlit rocks.

'It was scary,' Graham told us. 'It was a sign that Gaia was against the whole trip, and I saw dark spirits climbing on board – which is a really bad omen.'

He held my eye with his to convey that, as a spirit-child, a voyage of his would include experiential dimensions which would pass unnoticed on one of my own. He made the decision to turn back.

'I went downstairs for a torch, but couldn't find one, and by the time I got back on deck my friend had gone! I was calling him for ages, but there was no answer... so I decided to get help. I managed to steer back into the loch on my own, but it's weird because I was nearly back at the pontoon – like, an hour later – when I found my friend asleep on the cockpit floor...'

Graham gave us a significant look, just so that we would know to file the events of his voyage under the heading: *Unexplained.*

He put his boat up for sale after that, and never went to sea again.

After our own passage through the Dorus Mor, Linda and I held a roll-call and, finding all hands present, drifted into Loch Craignish, sails bellying as they cast long February shadows over the rippled water ahead. We watched the scenery – chains of long islets forming dorsal ridges on either side of the loch – pass us by in slow motion. Altering course to pass between the two rocks which guard the entrance to a lagoon brought the breeze onto our beam, and with that we fairly chomped through the gap before bearing off again toward the shore.

The water hereabouts is protected from the open sea by three off-lying islets, and a shelly spit. Even in a blow the waves which would threaten the tranquillity of the pool are tripped and tamed by the spit. Waves will break when the depth under them is less than three times their height; in three feet of water, only waves of less than a foot can pass over and into the pool beyond. A littering of disused mooring buoys gave the lagoon the appearance of an Olympic swimming pool marked off in lanes for racing, orange buoys bobbing like ballcocks. Three lonely yachts grouped together at the far end emphasised the surplus. We brought-up in shallow water over a stretch of clean sand and cast our anchor. Our troubles – or at least those

Goats at Kilchiaran

pertaining to the sea – were behind us. An unwonted trouble lay ahead.

The following day we'd just arrived back at our dinghy on the beach from a shopping trip with a great contribution to our summer stores bulging in countless plastic carrier bags, which cut into our hands, and turned them blue. The bus hadn't been able to take us the last mile to our boat, so we'd walked, then set down our load and straightened our backs with great sighs of relief, before untying our dinghy and dragging it to the water's edge to begin ferrying our shopping on board. On one of these sandy excursions we spotted a man we hadn't noticed until then. He was securing an inflatable dinghy to a post a short distance away, and seemed agitated. I always judge people by appearance – it's a fault in me. Because

he looked bad-tempered, I wanted to avoid him – yet there was nothing about him to suggest anything other than that he was the mildest-mannered man ever to scuttle a ship, or slit a throat. He was dressed – as any man would dress who lived alone in a house without mirrors – in a pair of green felt shorts held up with braces over a cheesecloth shirt, both of which his corporeal mass overflowed like a well-risen suet.

In Scotland it's considered bad manners not to acknowledge people you encounter, so we looked his way repeatedly in order to catch his eye, but he avoided those looks until we were just about to set off. You know how some folk have the knack of saying the exact opposite of what you're thinking?

'I should think you wanna talk to me...' he growled, then turned his back on us again in contempt.

I placed his accent as coming from somewhere near Hull, Yorkshire, as I walked over to him – a bit reluctantly – wearing what I hoped would be a placating smile.

'What about?'

'I expect you wanna ask me if you can pick up one of my moorings, doncha?'

We'd spent a thousand nights lying to our trusty anchor and had always woken to find our boat still lying in the same part of the world as we had left it – yet how did we know but that his mooring buoys were connected to the seabed on lengths of string?

'No, we're OK thanks.'

I've *heard* of people exploding with rage, but hadn't witnessed the phenomenon until then. There was no hanging around waiting for the fuse to burn with him. You had your result instantly.

'YOU'RE NOT "OK"!' he bellowed with spittle flying from his lips and leaping into the air like a frog in an electric storm. 'AND I'M TELLING YOU – YOU'D BETTER ASK ME IF YOU CAN PICK UP ONE OF MY MOORINGS!'

'But we don't need a mooring – we've got an anchor.'

'YOUR BOAT IS A BLOODY NUISANCE WHERE IT IS AND I'M TELLING YOU TO PICK UP ONE OF MY MOORINGS!'

I'd never met generosity like it, but finding it all a bit overwhelming, I turned to leave.

'ALL RIGHT! ALL RIGHT! YOU'VE ASKED FOR IT!' he said, picking things up from the ground, and throwing them down again. 'I'VE *TRIED* TO BE NICE... NOW WE'LL DO IT THE HARD WAY! YOU WAIT... YOU'LL SEE WHAT'LL HAPPEN TO YOU NOW!'

Just then I heard a voice speak and knew that the words it said would throw petrol onto the fire: '*Do you know,*' it said, '*you are the most* revolting *little man I've ever met.*'

I was just waiting to see how he would get on with that when I realised with a jolt that it was *I* who had spoken them. I don't know who was the more surprised, toad or me.

First he turned red, then blue. He spluttered and began waving his arms about, and at the same time his legs went into a kind of spasm, sending him leaping about uncontrollably in all directions.

Linda wasn't best pleased with me. She spoke my name in that cautionary tone she reserves for the times when I've been a very naughty boy. She placed herself between us and began shoving me down the beach.

As we rowed away the sound of his ranting and banging things about drifted out to us over the tranquil water. In an attempt to make things more unbearable for him I paused once or twice, allowing my oars to drip, and pretended to be struck by the beauty of the loch.

'What was that all about?' Linda asked when we got back on board.

'I have no idea.'

'Well, you've upset him.'

'He upset me first.'

As the days passed quietly by, and we waited to see what would befall us, we discovered in the lagoon an inexhaustible supply of mussels – smallish, but which could be gathered by the bucket-load simply by wading along the gravel shore at low water. I steamed them 'a la marinière', and we settled down to dinner with great hunks of buttered bread. At the very first bite we discovered that each mussel contained a dozen – sometimes as many as fifty – tiny pearls the size of the ball in a ballpoint pen. And it wasn't as if you could pull the mussel away and leave the pearls; the pearls were in the flesh of the mussels, making them like little bags of marbles. Not a single mussel was edible, and not a single pearl was a gem. We threw them overboard, sucking at our teeth.

Walking to the end of the peninsula and sitting at the water's edge, dazzled by the sun, we wondered if we could feel some warmth in the sun's rays... the warming rays of spring. The mirror of the sea was crystal clear. I noticed a movement out of the corner of my eye, and froze. Whatever it was disappeared, only to emerge again right between my legs, and I found myself face to face with an otter. We stared at one another. He pushed his nose an inch further forward, puzzled, sniffed at the air, and then realising what manner of beast I was, let out a gasp of surprise and shot below the water, splashing my trousers.

A pair of low stone-built cottages, long derelict, sat at the top of a beach enjoying remarkable views, south toward the sun, and the world. Each had just two rooms – one downstairs and one up a staircase set in the wall. At one time the pair had been one modest cottage, but had been made into two by building a massive stone wall down the middle. The cottages were not so far gone that they couldn't be made into a stunning house but the planning authority wouldn't allow it – we asked them.

On the way home, as we walked along the road, we surprised a husband and wife in the tiny front garden of their farmhouse as they made plans about what to plant this year. We hadn't seen them, and they hadn't seen us – separated as we were by an ornamental hedge.

We'd just come through a farm gate at the side of their house and it closed with a 'tink'. Mrs Farmer was the first to speak:

'Oooh!' she said, and Mr Farmer followed with: 'Oh!'

'Oh!' we replied.

The road was as quiet as a graveyard and we stood in it the better to see them.

'Well, it's a grand day!' observed Mr Farmer, opening with the Highland pleasantries which prelude every conversation.

'Yes! Yes!'

There was a short silence.

'And how are you today?' Mrs Farmer asked.

'Great thanks! How are you doing?'

Mr Farmer's white hair was crimped like the curly coat of a cat, and still had a faint tint of orange, indicating that when he was young it had been the colour of a mango. His wife was neatly preened, and dressed in starched linen.

For the next fifteen minutes we chatted in the road until the farmer's wife shivered and drew her shawl more closely about her shoulders, but the conversation was just getting going – they were as interested in our lifestyle living on board a boat as we were in theirs, beef farming in paradise.

'Would you have time for a cup of tea, and wee bite?' Mrs Farmer asked.

Moments later, seated on armchairs which had their floral upholstery protected by lacework on the arms and headrest, a tray of tea-things and fine china was set on the low table before us. The room – a small and spotless parlour – had a peat fire glowing in its hearth, and the loud, slow ticking of a mantelpiece clock, encased in wood, seemed to be keeping a record of how long we spent away from our work.

Two hours later, with darkness already gathering, we set off to walk home along a road which if anything was quieter than when we left it, and although the road was strange to us and this was the first time we ever walked along it, we had a feeling of being a part of the community – the words *There'll be a welcome in the Highlands* was made as clear to us, just then, as it could be.

I'd often been struck by something Frank Cowper said in his *Sailing Tours* when talking about 'the Scotch' as a race: *There is a prospect no doubt of much friendly intercourse with the natives, but the prospect hardly ever becomes a reality, and Scottish sympathies are much like the Scottish badge – a bristling thistle... I cannot say that Scottish sociability impressed itself strongly on my observation.*

Yet, everywhere we went, we found a warm welcome and a helping hand, and I wondered if Cowper spoiled it for himself – I found a clue to his personality when he gives advice to the Corinthian yachtsman on how he should conduct himself: *There is no harm in being polite,* he says, *without being at all deferential.*

Back in the days when we were building our boat, stick by stick, and quite naïve, we were given a piece of advice about living aboard from a man who'd just returned from a thirteen-year circumnavigation, and who'd come to dinner.

We opened the front door – we'd never met him before – to reveal a brooding man in his sixties, whose searching eyes looked us up and down, pityingly. We were in our thirties. He stepped in without speaking. Now we'd got him in the light we could see he'd had a fall – on one side, his clothes were muddy at the knee and elbow.

'You should put a light out back,' he informed us, irritably, 'for anyone arriving from that direction.'

Most of our visitors came via the front of the house – where the road was – but for reasons he didn't explain he'd come over the hill, through the wood, in the dark.

He spoke with bits of accent collected from all over the world, changing emphasis slightly to suit what he was saying: 'It's only thanks to my nivigation skills that I found you,' he told us, throwing in a bit of 'New Zealand'.

The evening was filled with tales of lonely, sometimes grim passages, followed by cloak-and-dagger arrivals in commercial ports where people hung about the wharfs throwing glances at his deck equipment, looking for an opportunity to improve their lot. And tales of working in diamond mines in South Africa – strip searches, and a prison regime.

'If ever you work in a diamond mine, the first money you earn, buy yourself a gun,' he advised me. 'You'll be working alongside some pretty hard bastards.'

Taking the evening as a whole, it didn't sound as though he had had a very lovely time. As he was leaving Linda asked, starry-eyed, if he had any advice for us. He had, and gave it to us in Afrikaans: 'Keep ya head darn and don't talk to innyone.' With that he pulled a hat low over his eyes, and left, heading for the back of the house.

It's the only advice we deliberately flout.

A man wearing a Tilley hat, driving a Volvo with a Canadian canoe on the roof, raised a hand in greeting as he passed me a few days later, as I walked along the road. He was wearing a tie. I'd never seen *anyone* wear a tie round here, and immediately wondered if he had anything to do with the fat man's threats. He had. Fifteen minutes later when I reached that part of the shore where my dinghy was beached, there was his car – *without* a canoe on its roof. I looked out to our boat and saw Linda sitting on deck apparently in conversation with someone on the far side. The tail end of a canoe came into view momentarily at our stern as it drifted back in the light airs, before pulling forward again. I couldn't hear any words, but the tones which drifted back to me were harmonious, so I walked on for an hour. They wouldn't need me, sticking my oar in.

He was from the Crown Estates Commission, Linda told me, responsible for the seabed. He'd been obliged to visit us in connection with a complaint he'd received about where we were anchored. Apparently, *most* of the complaints he received came from the man we privately called 'the toad' – though I don't think he called him that – and most of them were groundless. Their conversation had drifted into the more familiar channels of the story of our boat, where we hailed from, and how we lived. His parting words were that we shouldn't worry, but that he left it to our discretion to move our anchor thirty yards in any direction, to show willing. We didn't trouble ourselves to do that because we'd be moving it 500 miles before long.

At the marina, Mike was launching his boat. He watched from the shore as it was craned into the water, with one arm tucked behind his back, pulling little creases across the chest of his blue blazer, but instead of seizing this first opportunity to take the helm, he let the yardmen move it for him. He leaned toward me.

'This voyage doesn't merit the presence of a senior officer.' He winked. 'And if the paintwork gets scratched, it'll be on their insurance.' Then he bent his knees in a little bob of satisfaction.

He did take command of his vessel a couple of days later. It took four hours to load up all the gadgets he'd bought, punctuated every so often by a pair of hands emerging through his hatch, pulling something off the pile, and then disappearing to search for a place to stow it. At last when the cockpit was clear and all the lines and sails had been checked a dozen times – and the spanking-new outboard had proved itself by idling for an hour without missing a beat – they prepared to make a departure from the cloud of blue fumes.

'Now we'll see how the Navy does it...' I said to Linda as Mike settled himself at the helm and assumed a lofty air. 'Take note.'

'CAST OFF!' Mike called in a voice that could be heard among the mountains to his girlfriend, who was sitting beside him.

'What... let the ropes off?'

He nodded once. She untied the forward line, and wandered back with it in her hands.

'NOT THAT ONE!' he yelled, as though someone had unplugged a life-support machine. She untied the 'other' line.

'GET ON BOARD!' he called as the boat began to drift away.

His girlfriend looked at the gap, and hesitated.

'JUMP!'

She wasn't sure if she could make it.

'FOR CHRIST'S SAKE – JUMP!'

With a shriek she leapt the short distance from the pontoon and landed in the rigging, panting like a storm-blown bird.

'They're in for a nice time,' Linda said.

9 MY INHERITANCE FROM SIR FRANCIS CHICHESTER

THE FAERY ISLES LIVE UP TO THEIR NAME. The inner pool is guarded by one of the tightest entrances on the west coast of Scotland – a narrow gap through a canyon of rock, one side showing above water, one below. We punted ourselves through with an oar. It had become a favourite haunt of ours and although we'd never seen anyone else here, someone must use it from time to time because there's a buoy at one end of it, close to the forest shore. Today, something was tied to the buoy – we could see it floating water-logged alongside. I rowed over, wondering if I'd find a cache of drugs, but when I got there I found the dead body of a seal whose back flippers had become entangled in the underwater 'riser' rope which was attached to the seabed. The rope had trapped him so that he could just reach the surface at low water, but not at high water. I noticed a gaping wound in his back pecked open by gulls. Somehow his lonely death emphasised the loneliness of this wild spot. As I rowed away I tried not to think how the seal must have struggled, or whether its fate would have been any different if we'd arrived a day or two earlier.

We'd asked the post office in nearby Tayvallich if they'd hold a parcel for us 'Poste Restante'. Some post offices like to see you arrive, and then leave, but the post office at Tayvallich like to hang on to you and make a fuss of you. They have a coffee room which looks out over the water at boats dozing at their moorings. Affable smiling staff, confident of the quality of their wares, chat amongst themselves, providing a backdrop of soundbites of village life, a hum of activity which is only suspended whenever a new gateau is unwrapped and placed on display, allowing a frisson of excitement to pass through the room like a Mexican wave. There turned out to be three bulky parcels for us, and if the staff were pleased to have got shot of them at last, they didn't show it.

Our wooden decks had been bothering us for years, leaking every time it rained. The worst month for them was September, after a hot summer sun has been burning down onto them (sometimes they got so hot you could fry an egg on them). The boards shrink and the first torrential downpour of autumn finds out all its cracks, and drips down onto us in our bed. It's miserable. We thought we'd tried everything – and the only difference between one product and another was how long it was before they failed. A lot of wooden-boat owners paint their decks with a grey anti-slip paint which seals any leaks, but we couldn't bear to cover our lovely wood. At last we overcame our meanness and invested a thousand pounds into a product we'd heard good reports of – Coelan – which looks like varnish but stretches like rubber. Living up to the letter of the instructions to paint it onto bone-dry wood was going to be a tall order in Scotland, in March – yet not a drop of rain fell from the cirrostratus nebulosus as the first coat went on. We rigged up some tarpaulins, which turned out to be just as well because we had a rogue shower overnight.

On the third of the four days it took us to complete the treatment, to our astonishment a boat – another yacht – came into the pool in which we had never seen another living soul. And us looking like the poor relations to some boat refugees. He set his anchor. He looked rather stern. We didn't speak.

During the night the wind picked up to a near gale, arriving from the only direction to which the anchorage was exposed. Our tarpaulin woke us at four, flogging wildly. The cracking noise was made worse by echoing off the clifflets close by, and I suspect our neighbour was beginning to regret coming here. We had to move or our tarpaulins would be torn to shreds. We couldn't take the tarps off because there were spots of rain in the air and the deck would get wet, so at first light we devised a scheme whereby I'd be on the tiller, blind under the canvas, and Linda would stand with her head poking out through the tarps, calling out directions. I knew my way out of the anchorage by watching the depth sounder – there was a little hole three feet deeper than anywhere else situated near the entrance and I knew if I could find that, I could find the underwater channel which led out. But in order to find my hole I had to steer toward a rocky islet first. It was a sound navigational plan which Francis Chichester taught the world in 1931 when he was flying solo across the Tasman Sea and needed to find Norfolk Island. In those days, if you flew 600 miles out to sea looking for a dot of land, and when you'd done your 600 miles it wasn't there, the only possible explanation is that you'd been blown sideways, and the question most on your mind is whether to turn left or right in order to resolve the problem. One will lead to the island, the other will lead you to your death, as there isn't enough fuel to return home.

What Chichester did was to set off from the mainland deliberately steering a few degrees 'off course' (to the right, it may have been) so that when he'd flown his 600 miles he knew that if he turned 90 degrees to the left, sooner or later he'd find Norfolk Island. And he did. Had he failed, he and his 'off course' navigational invention would have died before they both had a chance to become famous.

I once met Francis Chichester's son, Giles, in his capacity of chairman of the family map business in London, and failed to sell him a new telephone system for his office, even though his office needed one. Badly. But I've never held the telephone incident against the family and don't have the slightest hesitation in paying Chichester Senior the compliment of copying his navigation methods: so like him I deliberately steered 'off-course' – though in my case that meant I was aiming *for* the islet, as mentioned.

My eyes burned into the depth sounder to know how much water we had under us. And in any case it was *all* I could see as I was flying by my instruments alone. Suddenly I heard a warning blast from a ship's horn so violently loud that I thought the *Queen Mary* was approaching full-steam ahead, and we were just feet from impact. It vibrated through me, rattling the crockery, and shattered one of our finest Ming vases. Clawing at the walls of my tent in a blind panic, I saw to my surprise the blast came not from the *Queen Mary*, but from the squiffy little boat with whom we'd shared our anchorage. Its owner stood on the foredeck holding a fog horn the size of a fire extinguisher over his head, and still wearing yesterday's stern expression. Strewn around his feet his crew were arranged very much as Jesus had His disciples arranged whilst they posed for John Singleton Copley as he painted his masterpiece *Ascension*. Seeing my face appear through the tarps, our saviour threw his arm heavily to the left, indicating the direction I was to follow which would take me to the entrance/exit of the pool. Had he never *heard* of Francis Chichester? As we drifted along the 'deep' water channel, as witnessed by the echo-sounder, I parted the walls of the tent for one last glance of the man and his foghorn, and saw him nodding his reluctant approval at our having followed his advice.

A couple of miles away we found shelter in the lee of a tree-clad hill, threw out our anchor once more, and put on the last two coats of treatment. Next day we took off the tarps, and prayed for rain. When it began to fall, it continued in torrents for 36 hours, but not a drop came below. We couldn't quite believe what we were seeing.

With luxury accommodation to offer our friend Lindy and her new husband, they included us as part of their honeymoon tour of Scotland. We'd arranged to meet them in Tayvallich, where they pulled alongside us standing in the verge of the road. They were trailing one of those caravans that look like a brushed aluminium rugby ball on wheels and used to be popular in America in the 1960s. A pile of sleeping bags, clothing, walking boots and a frying pan, which teetered in a heap on the back seat, collapsed over them when Tim, recognising us, stood on the brake and brought his vehicle to a standstill.

Lindy began jabbing her finger against the window, trying to say something above the strains of an orchestra blaring out from the CD player. In her rush to get to us she became entangled in the seatbelt and fought to release herself. When she was free from that tangle, the door wouldn't open. When it did, she fell on all fours at our feet, followed by a map, a half-eaten apple, a clog, and a pair of French knickers.

Lindy's greetings are an irresistible force – they fling open the gates of your heart. She has an unshakeable faith in the goodness of people. There's *nothing* you can do to put her straight on that one. She cradled our faces in her hands, blinking at us as though we were somehow wonderful.

'Oh my darlings!' she gasped, her eyes magnified behind owly glasses, the arms of which disappeared into wild grey hair.

'*God* it's s-o-o-o lovely to see you! Let me have a look at you...'

In the driver's seat Tim, it seems, had been getting stressed – he'd been following the same single track road through a forest for eight miles, convinced they were going the wrong way.

A few years younger than Lindy, he was self-conscious, reserved. When there were absolutely no more switches for him to turn off he stepped onto the road and walked the long way round, appearing from the back of the caravan dressed in zebra-print trousers.

'*Hel-l-lo!!*' he called, as though we were the last people he expected to find there.

Lindy's greetings go on for a while, so Tim filled the next five minutes by disappearing and then reappearing from the back of his caravan, calling out a new remark with each appearance: 'Wonderful!' 'Lovely...' '*So* nice.'

'Are you enjoying your honeymoon?' Linda asked, at last.

There was a silence.

'Erm...' said Lindy, trailing off.

Tim, realising how this was beginning to sound, came to the rescue. 'Well...' he said, positively, then dried up.

They looked at each other with forgiving smiles.

We ferried them and their belongings out to our boat anchored over her own reflection, amid scenery as grand as Scotland can make it. We brewed a pot of tea, sat in the cockpit, and ate a slice of the wedding cake they'd brought along, absorbed by the atmosphere of the boating life. We hadn't been able to make it to their wedding in the barns of an historic farmhouse on Exmoor, but our friend JFW had.

'I was the only one wearing trousers,' he told us. 'I hadn't realised everyone was going in robes. And if I had, I don't even know where you're s'posed to go to *buy* white robes. So I wore trousers... and a shirt, of course. It wasn't like any other wedding I've been to. Me and Jenny were late because at the last minute Tim asked us to buy him some white underpants and we had to drive all the way to Barnstable to get them, which was a complete waste of our journey because *white* underpants are a mistake with a *white* robe (you can see them through the robe) – what he *should* have asked us to get were *flesh-coloured* underpants. By the time we arrived we found all the men standing at the top of a hill, waving branches in the air, howling. The women were in the valley below. Suddenly the men rushed down on them, waving their branches and shouting. Tim grabbed Lindy – rather roughly, I thought – and led her through some arches. It was a civil ceremony. And it rained.'

With that JFW had recalled all the pertinent facts about the day.

'Was it fun?' we asked.

'It was...' – there was a long pause – '...extraordinary.'

After tea we set off back to the Faery Isles – which no nature lover could fail to enjoy – just a couple of miles away, at the head of the loch. Fingers of bare rock reached out to us as we motored past, and wherever that rock attained an elevation of two or three metres, dense forests of gnarled oak grew. The forest floor was lent a mystical appearance by its litter of twisted roots, which rose up in hoops, wearing a carpet of soft green moss.

When we slid through the canyon entrance to our favourite anchorage *this* time, we were under sail – showing off, drifting

An island to oneself

between the reefs, propelled by the softest of winds. Two walkers were sitting on a rock at the water's edge on one of the islets, open mouthed. We passed within ten feet of them.

'It gets rather shallow in here, you know...' they warned.

'Yes – thanks! We've been in here before...'

It seemed strange to be holding a conversation 'under sail' with someone on the shore. We'd disturbed their tranquillity, and when Tim started shouting, it wasn't long before they left in search of somewhere quiet. No sooner had our anchor rattled to the seabed than he suddenly appeared on deck, naked. He screamed a primordial scream, and then leapt over the side and into the water. Its coldness seemed to quieten him down – which I found reassuring – and it helped to remember that, as a psychiatrist, he represented the rational side of society.

Doing faint little breaststrokes at the surface, I noticed he'd turned blue and was blowing like a man drowning. He made for the front of the boat, then the back, and then stopped in confusion and asked which was the best way to get back on board. Good question. We hadn't been faced with that problem before.

10 THE CHILD PIRATES OF PENZANCE

WE BEGAN OUR JOURNEY SOUTH. The island of Gigha is widely used by yachtsmen as the hopping-off as well as the point of arrival for Scotland. Accordingly it was the last Scottish place we visited. Ireland's north coast, twenty miles from here, has strong tides around its headlands, which it's important to get right – by leaving from Gigha's Ardminish Bay you can time your arrival at those headlands perfectly. We hadn't expected to see many boats in the bay, yet it was packed. Amongst them Linda spotted a familiar hull. We rowed over.

Ten years earlier, long before we had even started building our boat, we'd read about a chap who'd built a number of steel yachts in the style of a boat known as the Spray – made famous a hundred years ago as the first boat to sail around the world single-handed. We were thinking about building a steel Spray ourselves, and had managed to find Paul Fay and his boat, all those years ago, overwintering in a river on the North Devon coast. Arriving unannounced to pick his brains about building such a boat, we'd knocked on his hull to be welcomed by the same startled expression he wore today. We reminded him and his wife, Mo, of how we'd met, how we'd shared fish and chips together, and how we'd pumped them for advice. At last they recognised us and invited us on board to catch up on news.

They'd both been 'lone' sailors with ocean crossings under their keels, but now sailed together aboard their latest self-built boat, with lots of light and a homely layout to the accommodation. They use a 'junk' rig, which is even rarer these days than the gaff, and based on technology five thousand years older. It's also the rig, according to Gavin Menzies in his fascinating book, *1421 – The Year China Discovered the World*, which first took man around the world. It seems strange to bump into friends you haven't seen for years, in tiny harbours hundreds of miles from where you last met – yet within minutes it seemed only yesterday that we were last together.

The following morning with a north-westerly wind to blow us along our southerly course, we set off running along the coast of the Mull of Kintyre, evenly balanced between the excitement of the journey ahead and the sadness of what we were leaving behind. Who knows when we would see again that hallmark of the Scottish coast – black-brown mountains rising sheer out of the water. In the North Channel the seas became lively to let us know that great stirrings were going on in the ocean below. A traffic-separation scheme for the use of large shipping takes all the best water for itself in the North Channel and shoves we small-boaters into boiling overfalls, easily provoked by wind, spring tides, and changes of direction around the Mull. The tide beneath our keel, flowing fast, sped us south.

Out there in the thick of it, whilst foaming waves dashed against our hull, I noticed my fishing rod jump, and bend to a heavy catch. I'd put an animated lure over the side to drag through the water in the hope of catching a bass. An old encyclopaedia of fishing we have on board says that '...these fish are not to be found much north of Cornwall'. Yet I'd heard that they had been caught in Northern Ireland – perhaps climate change had extended their range? I was a long time winding my fish in because it was so heavy, and we were sailing fast as we rose and fell over the eddies, with gusts of wind coming and going so that I had to drop the rod sometimes and grab the helm, which needed both hands to hold it.

Eventually, having got the line close astern, my catch broke through the surf and I saw to my horror that I had caught not a fish but a gannet. When these birds spot fish swimming near the surface they do a barrel-roll, inverting themselves in flight, and dive, hitting the water like a missile. He'd been fooled by my lure. Although it was alive when I got it close astern, giving one or two exhausted flaps of its wings, and looking at me so that I felt sick with remorse, it drowned before I could get it on board, finally expiring next to me in the cockpit. With hindsight, had I tried mouth-to-mouth resuscitation I might have saved it.

We felt guilty entering Larne Lough, swanning about on a pleasure boat, because on all sides of us real work was being done. Ferries towered over us to starboard, embarking passengers and vehicles for Stranrear, and to port, the great chimneys of a power station belched their smoke busily. Ahead of us stood cylinders for gas storage. But Larne Lough is a great place to drop the anchor overnight on account of its distance from the North Channel, the ease with which you can get in, and how protected it feels once your anchor is down. Beyond the 'commercial area', anchorages lie both to the east and to the west within a few metres. It wasn't the best view we'd ever had – even the Almanac describes it in a *but you wouldn't want to go there* sort of tone, yet Frank Cowper, writing in 1895 – presumably before the power station was built – thought that in some ways Larne Lough was *'the best little harbour in the whole of the Irish Seas'*.

Heading south from Larne Lough, and only a mile or two along the way, lies the Isle of Muck, which always frightens me. It's a bleak rock sticking sheer out of the water surrounded by angry foam, and is separated from the mainland by only a couple of hundred metres. As you approach, it looks as though you can slip past it in the calm water inshore, but you can't. Or perhaps open-boat fishermen can, who know the place rock by rock. To seaward there is deep water right up to the cliff-face, which tempts me in close when I think of the fish that must be living there. Dreams of catching a whopper overcome my presentiment that something bad is about to happen. There is a strange atmosphere as we close in, tension in the air, as though a glass was about to shatter. And when I cast my line toward the rock it is swallowed insignificantly and without a splash by the mauve water. The shriek of a gull wheeling overhead echoes back almost immediately from the cliff, warning me I have approached too close-in. I threw the tiller over, and headed offshore.

Six miles later we opened-up Belfast Lough and the protection we'd been enjoying from the land so close to windward suddenly vanished. We began to heave over short waves. A wreck-fishing boat which must have been anchored in water half a mile deep fired up its engine, motored around behind us as we passed, and when he'd finished catting his anchor the skipper sat on the foredeck to face us, and give us a hearty wave. We and they, being on slightly diverging courses, allowed plenty of time for lingering glances, and as the distance between us grew we sketched each other's lives in thought.

A cargo vessel two or three miles away on our left was worrying us: would she pass ahead, astern, or sink us in her great bow wave? That question was settled when a pilot boat zoomed out from Belfast to meet her, crossed our bow, and then the pair of them slowed down as they met. We watched the pilot boat kiss the larger vessel in greeting, and as she did so a man leapt onto a rope ladder dangling over the side of the ship, climbed on board, strode purposefully up to the bridge, and began to pilot the vessel into harbour.

We usually pass inside Copeland Island through the Donaghadee (Donadee) Sound to save a detour offshore. Here the sea loses its deep-water blue suddenly and becomes shallow-water brown. The change happens so quickly it fills us with misgivings about our decision to have come this way at all. The tide runs fast, keeps odd hours, and flows diagonally across the channel, setting mariners onto the shoals. We seem to be the only people to use this route. Everyone else either goes round or goes into Portavogie, halfway along the route. We thought of popping into Portavogie once but the Almanac put us off; in our mind's-eye we imagined a tiny harbour overfilled with people wading, or splashing around in dinghies.

Instead we carried on for Ardglass, where we arrived at low water to be greeted by the sight and smell of fresh seaweed hanging on wet rocks which seemed to stretch up to the sky. If someone had yelled at that moment we would have turned and run – if there was *room* to turn. Cowper didn't go in – he excused himself by saying that he passed close enough to *look* in and saw that it was full of fishing boats, so went on. I think his courage failed him, though yachts didn't have engines in those days, and the twists and turns we had to make to get into our berth were so tight that even *with* an engine we didn't do it very well. We didn't hit anyone, but there were a couple of nine-point turns. No one came to help us – well, you don't like to, do you, when you see people making complete fools of themselves?

The following afternoon a boat we recognised came into the harbour. It looked slightly tired, as boats do when they have completed at least one circumnavigation, and as soon as we saw the boat's name we knew we weren't mistaken. We'd last seen her 300 miles and several years ago, in Cornwall, and leapt off our boat to trot along the pontoons, take his lines, and greet him, calling as we went: 'John! John!'

When he didn't answer I put my hands to my mouth in the shape of a shouting-trumpet.

Linda stopped me. 'Don't forget he's deaf.'

'Mm? Oh, of course.'

So we walked toward him, looking sheepish and raising our eyebrows every time he glanced in our direction.

'Ah!' he said at last, throwing us his lines. 'Nice to see you both! How are you?'

'Great, thanks! As soon as we saw you come in we recognised your boat – the name is unmistakable!'

'Eh?'

Greetings would have to wait a minute. John's a good lip-reader close-to; at a distance it has to be 'signing', in lieu of which all we could do was hold up bits of rope and point to dockside cleats enquiringly. On board his boat we were beaten back by the smell of leaking diesel – Linda wasn't too bad with it, but I had to sit outside where there was still some oxygen in the air. I mentioned it to John, but he only sniffed at the air and looked at me as though I was imagining things.

He'd been on passage for a couple of days and hadn't had a chance to get to the shops.

'Do you mind your tea black, only the milk's gone off?' He glooped a few lumps of it into a glass and held it up as proof. 'Or perhaps you don't mind it like that?'

'Black please,' we chimed.

'I've got loads of sugar... you can have as much of that as you like.'

'Just black, please.'

He pushed aside some vintage tourist office leaflets which were scattered on the saloon table and made space for the mugs.

'Fraid I haven't got any biscuits. Ooh, saying that, I could make some toast-and-relish.'

Leaping to his feet, brimming with hospitality, he immediately set-to, unable to hear us urging him not to trouble. As he worked he narrated his actions like a TV chef, but with his back turned, he was oblivious to the effect he was having on his audience.

'Now, this bread is a bit stale, but it's not mouldy or anything, and when it's toasted you won't notice the difference.' He threw us a smile, as though that was a culinary secret which he passed on as a gift.

'I've only got one tin of anchovies, but I'll make it go further by mixing it with a tube of tomato puree and some brown sauce. Do you like brown sauce?' he asked, throwing another glance over his shoulder, but not waiting for the answer.

'Now then, how are these doing?'

He pulled out the toast to inspect them – nothing had happened yet. 'Toast takes ages on this cooker. How do you do toast on your boat?'

'With difficulty.'

'Pardon?'

'With difficulty.'

'Don't think I've got one of those. Now then... is there any margarine left?'

He found the margarine, opened the lid, looked inside, gave it a sniff, pulled a doubtful face, sniffed again, and then shrugged as though he was prepared to give it the benefit of the doubt. Whilst John mashed the anchovies into the brown sauce with the back of a fork, I noticed that Linda was looking at me. We exchanged a polite smile.

Before long the toast-and-relish was set before us.

'There! I hope that's all right... I think it is, anyway. So – where are you heading?'

The intense flavours, the nagging doubt, and the atmosphere, which hung with oil, made for a very memorable tea.

The sea between Ardglass and Dublin is remarkable for having almost no tidal stream, so for once in our lives we didn't have to time our departure. But because the sea hereabouts doesn't move much it seems to have grown viscous over time, and is a right bastard to sail through. Many a lively day our boat has skipped along at seven – even eight – knots for hour after hour. But in the stretch of water between Ardglass and Dublin – a distance of 60 tedious miles – we've never achieved four knots, no matter how hard we've spurred her on. We endured the passage taking everything as a personal slight against us. The course took us well offshore, and in any case the coast hereabouts is flat and monotonous; for relief, you face aft from time to time, in order to admire the Mourn mountains which you are leaving behind.

Sailing between Dublin and Arklow in late summer a few years previously we'd seen smoke billowing off the land so profusely that it seemed the whole of Ireland was on fire, yet it was only farmers burning stubble after the harvest. We were sailing too early in the year to enjoy that diversion, and breathe in the smoky fragrances which floated out to us across three miles of water, entangled with salt and seaweed, and so endured a second dull passage on an overcast and peevish day with not much to see. The exception being Wicklow Head, the nose of which poked out across our course. If the water between Ardglass and Dublin is viscous, the water around Wicklow Head is thin and lively – assuming the results of our survey of four visits can be relied upon. And there's a helluva keen yacht-racing club somewhere around Wicklow. Each time we've gone round – whether north or south – we've found ourselves meandering along like Breton farmers selling onions from a bicycle when the Tour de France comes along. Suddenly a hundred boats with Kevlar sails appear alongside, skimming over the water with their decks awash, and moments later leave us behind, bobbing about in their foam. In spite of the bracing conditions around Wicklow Head the crews of the race boats almost look as if they're enjoying themselves. But of course they know they'll be standing in front of a pint of beer in less than an hour, whereas we'll be lucky if we're in before dark.

We went into Arklow, which had become a favourite – there's plenty of room for yachts in the River Avoca, but we always turn left into the fishing harbour. I don't know why – it's oily, dirty and smells of rotting whelks, but hey-ho, it's the genuine article. We tied up to one of its rusting hulks.

Mooring post

Shortly afterwards a German yacht came in and motored around the four-square of the harbour, her skipper throwing doubtful glances before steering for the exit. Arklow in general, and James the Harbour Master in particular, welcomes yachts, so I whistled to the German boat in case he was thinking of leaving, and indicated to him that if he was worried about getting oily fenders he was welcome to tie alongside us. He, his wife and daughter were circumnavigating Britain anticlockwise, and when they learned that we knew Cornwall pretty well asked us – if they had time for only *one* stop – where we would recommend. The Scilly Islands, we sang out, unanimously, and in particular The Cove, which lies between the islands of Agnes and Gugh. It's risky to make recommendations because everyone's tastes are so different, but he'd asked for our opinion, and that was it. Fortunately he'd spotted the Scillies on the chart before meeting us and had been half-wondering if they might be worth the detour – our recommendation settled the matter for him.

The run between Arklow and Kilmore Quay is filled with interest, particularly because the tide runs fast, helping you along, but at a slight angle to the narrow lanes that form the inshore passage between sandy shoals on either side, on which the sea breaks. It's impossible not to wonder what would happen to your yacht, as you pass by these banks, if you happened to ground on one. The pictures presented to our minds filled us with morbid feelings of utter desolation. Consequently we took a particularly keen interest in the navigation just here. The distance between the navigational buoys which mark the passage is often more than three miles – that's about the distance between our eye and the horizon – so the day was spent in 'looking out', spotting them, and, having spotted them, watching them in case they slipped away. A high-speed ferry, capable of more than 30 knots, operating from Rosslare, crossed our path at the very point where suddenly there were five navigational marks crammed into a mile of water, all of which had to be identified in order to know how to proceed. The visibility was hazy, so that everything appeared amorphous and grey. But once we were round the corner and sailing along the south coast, the weather brightened. Or was it we who brightened?

Kilmore Quay welcomes all-comers, but it's a tiny harbour which, owing to its location on the south-east tip of Ireland, gets very crowded with both commercial and pleasure craft. We arrived at 8pm, picked our way between the trawlers, and tied up alongside a spanking charter yacht, arousing curiosity and suspicion amongst its well-heeled yachters in equal measure. On the one hand they wanted to mug-along with salty-looking folk like ourselves, and on the other they didn't. There was a trawler at our stern, tied to the quay wall, which together with several others worked through the night, repairing gear under dazzling deck lights, and with their engines running to generate power, so we didn't sleep at all. In lieu of mooring fees which we didn't want to pay we reluctantly put a fiver in an envelope to appease our feeling of guilt, stuffed it through the letterbox of the unmanned office, and motored out of the harbour at half-five the next morning. Some places are so noisy that it's not until you leave them that you remember that some places aren't.

The wind had been blowing from the north west at sixes and sevens for a couple of days, and was still blowing at seven when we left Ireland for the Scillies, 130 miles away. We reckon on covering 100 miles a day, but today we might do better. Out in St George's Channel, heading south, we were creaming over the rolling waves. The wind was forecast to settle down to Force Four later in the day, and the noisy trawler men had done us a favour by starting us off early. Twelve miles out, Linda's face appeared through the hatch.

'Alfie, I'm not happy.'

'What do you mean?'

'It's too rough.'

'Do you want to turn back?'

'What do you think?'

'If you want to turn back we might as well do it now as later.'

'OK, then.'

'Mind you, we can't go back to Kilmore Quay because we've underpaid them... We'll have to head for Dunmore East.'

'OK, then.'

Sailing downwind in strong winds is noticeably more comfortable than sailing upwind in them. Linda put her head out of the hatch again.

'Alfie, is this all right?'

'Yes, and you're going to have to put up with it for a couple of hours until we get back in the lee of land.'

Two and a half hours later we regained the protection of the coast; the seas fell flat, and the wind, as forecast, died down. Linda's face appeared back in the hatch.

'What's happened to the wind?'

'It's died down – like the forecast said it would.'

She looked around at the flat sea, and the land close by.

'Then why have we turned back?'

There are times when I'm speechless – that was one of them.

For the second time that day, five hours after the first, we left Ireland and rolled on our way over waves which wore flashing white smiles in the brilliant sun. For most of that day I could only mourn the labour lost, and dream of where we would be 'now' if we hadn't turned back.

Boats are great places to live, great ways to see the coast, but for me, I have to confess, not a great means of transport if there are distances to be covered. I prefer the exploring to the travelling. Journeys by boat are slow, and watching the mast swing its way across the sea is like watching the moment hand of a watch whilst you wait for a week to expire. Having said that, seeing land grow before you on the distant horizon is mesmerisingly interesting. It fills out its contours and seems to acquire personality layer by layer, like new embryonic life. The newborn Isles of Scilly began to fill our horizon. Round Island Light rose modestly above a scattering of islands, on each of which we could imagine what was going on right now. Our minds turned to what we would do first, whether to anchor in Grimsby Sound close by the rock and fern of Tresco, and what we would say to Henry the Harbour Master, or whether we would press on for Agnes, and have a pint in the Turk's Head gazing out at the loveliest pub-view in Britain.

It occurred to me that the rock which stands sentry to New Grimsby Sound, between the islands of Tresco and Bryher, bluff and black as it is, seems rather small to hold back the mighty Atlantic. In fact, taken as a whole the Scillies – which are just a scattering of low-lying rocks twenty-odd miles offshore, boomed by waves which are meeting their first obstruction for 3,000 miles – seem to have done rather well not to have been swallowed up by the seas. Yet as soon as you come within the Sound, the wind falls light and the sea is tamed to a smooth swell. From a perch on the cliff above, a herring gull spread his wings, swept down the face of the rock, and passed low over our deck to know if we'd been a-fishing. He acts as a kind of customs officer for the gulls on the island, on the lookout for fish offal being brought to these shores – if you have any, a single shriek alerts every gull within the port authority to swarm about you. If you're clean, he says nothing, and rides the wind like a high-speed elevator back up to his observation post, where he touches lightly down, and folds the wings he didn't beat once.

Something about the Scilly Isles announces that you are on holiday – the sun, the sand, the solitude. We glided through the sound with its line of *heavy* mooring buoys. 'You'll always be safe, but you won't always be comfortable...' Henry will tell you if you pick one up, and wonder if you'll be 'all right'.

Preparing to sail off a buoy

The allusion is to the rolling swell, which the rocks cannot prevent from passing among and between the islands, and which keeps yachts' masts swaying like metronomes. It was a bit rolly now, which decided us to pass onwards to the interior 'lagoon', zigzagging our way between the reefs and shoals, which can only be taken near high water, and which claim a low-water victim every few days in the height of summer, usually to refloat harmlessly on the next tide. We passed the island of St Mary's, not stopping for anything until we reached the object of our desire: The Cove – an anchorage of such impossible summer loveliness that it would serve well as a cover illustration for *Five Go Down to the Sea*. The Cove is formed by a sand bar between the islands of St Agnes and Gugh which covers at high water springs, and only then can they be said to be two islands.

On busy days in the summer, The Cove might play host to 50 boats – we made 51. But the folks who get there first always leave a space for us next to the rocks, and we find it as comfortable a berth as any. Twelve of the boats were French, and there, amongst the crowd of masts, we saw a German flag. We recognised the boat we had met at Arklow, flattered that they had acted on our advice, and hopeful that they were pleased they did. We rowed over and were invited on board. They hadn't put into any harbour between Arklow and here, sailing instead through the strong winds. They'd had a bit of a hammering, and torn a sail. The weather now was better than perfect, and we hoped it had all been worthwhile.

'What do you think of the anchorage?' we asked.

'Dis,' said Mr Germany, speaking in a voice which permits no contrary opinions, 'is der British Krown-Jewel!'

We always overstay our welcome in the Scillies. Not that the islanders let you know when it's time for you to move on. The weather does that. The wind had been rising steadily for a few days, forcing all visiting yachts to congregate in the same small sheltered anchorages – space was at a premium, tension in the air. At sunrise one morning a boat owned by a friend of ours from Falmouth dragged its anchor, bringing rebuke from his neighbours who blamed him just then for everything that was wrong in their lives. His was a small boat by comparison with the cruisers which usually visit the Scillies. Size matters and the skipper of a smaller boat is somehow assumed to be less competent and more of a nuisance than the skipper of a bigger one. His neighbours suspected him of being a novice, out of his depth. In truth his experience exceeded all of ours put together, being crew on one of the Falmouth Pilot Boats and practically living at sea. Overnight his wife had been feeling seasick, so he rowed her and their daughter ashore so that they could 'go home' by ferry, leaving him to sail home alone. At his request I held his tiller and motored ahead whilst he heaved up his anchor, then he took the helm from me, dropped me off back on board my boat, and set off to sail the 70 miles home in near-gale winds, past the graveyards of Land's End and the Lizard. Off Land's End his jib blew to shreds in a squall. He mentioned the fact with an 'inconvenient' roll of his eyes when we saw him a week later back in Falmouth, when he rewarded me for my paltry help by dropping a carrier-bag full of scallops on deck, shells snapping shut every time you peered-in at them. The generosity of the Cornish is equalled only by the kindness of Scots.

On our own voyage home from the Scillies we stopped to visit Mousehole (rendered locally as *Marsel*). Approaching the aptly-named harbour gives you the impression that you are sailing into a cartoon – it's one of those charming and historic villages on the Cornish coast which wouldn't have been possible with town planning, and could only have grown organically. As we approached late in the afternoon of a hot day, the harbour was thronging. Colourful boats bobbed at their moorings, swimmers filled the spaces between them, and children ran along the massive harbour walls which in the winter protected the village from even the worst storm (unless there's much east in it). Our approach toward the harbour was a call to action. Boys sitting on the beach threw half-eaten ice creams backwards over their shoulders and swarmed onto the harbour walls to defend their port against incoming pirates. From there they hurled abuse at us, threw fists in the air, wielding sticks in the other hand, and turned into reality all the chaotic action they'd previously been heroically imagining would be their part in the event of an invasion. Somewhere in their heads a klaxon was going off with the warning:

Attention! This is not a rehearsal! One urchin of about ten, a self-elected champion, stood yelling at us from above the harbour entrance as we were about to pass through and, when that failed to stop us, hit upon a clever idea. He leaped off the wall straight into our path, hoping to stop us by triggering our adult instinct to protect children from harm.

What he couldn't have known was that although the skipper of the pirate ship didn't like children, he was a tireless defender of their right to learn by experience. On top of the wall the child was insuperable. Swimming in front of our bow as it cut its way through the water toward him, he was wide-eyed with terror. He floated like a cork and flapped his arms so fast it was a wonder he didn't take off. In spite of the pleading and remorseful glances he threw my way I pretended not to see him at all. By now, at the writing of these words, that child will be a charming young man, quietly grateful for the small help I rendered him in forming his pleasing personality.

Mousehole is so small that we wondered if we'd get in. Once in, our thoughts turned immediately to whether we'd get out. It's tiny, and shallow, like a child's paddling pool – littered with swimmers in arm bands splashing about on lilos. We only had time to smell the air, with its suntan lotion, beer and chips, and notice that every eye in the harbour was on us before deciding to leave, if such a thing was possible. Seeing that we were constrained by our draft, other mariners paddled their lilos away, allowing us to swing ship. The water was so clear that we could see the cat's-cradle of frape moorings laid out on the bottom – and so shallow that our propeller threw up great clouds of sand, obscuring them, as it worked hard to turn our lumbering mass in a pirouette. I thought I was going to make an ass of myself by gathering some of the moorings in the prop, at which we would have been trapped, allowing the children to make a final and decisive assault. In the event we executed a rather amateurish thirteen-point turn and left with all the dignity we could muster.

We imagined that Falmouth would be thrilled to see its wanderers return when we came dashing into the harbour a few days later, determined to put on a show. We positively flew in under a braggish amount of sail in a press of wind and rounded up noisily just off the town quay, at which I rushed forward to lower away the anchor as the vessel slowed under shaking canvas. The anchor clanged over the roller, there was a splash, and the chain rattled down after it. At the same time I heard a shout go up from the land behind me and, with both hands full, turned to see what the matter was. On the quay a father and his son of about 12 – both of them strangers to us – rushed to the railings cheering and clapping above their heads in an unbridled appreciation of the spectacle. We were home!

11 SCHOONER SKIPPER'S SUPPER SCUPPERED

WHENEVER SOMEONE IN THE STREET RECOMMENDS the brand of varnish we should use, a crowd gathers round and an argument breaks out which only comes to an end when everyone is punch-drunk, and too hoarse to shout. It's the same with antifouling, and the reason so much passion is wasted on them is that nothing really works.

We use a well-known copper/epoxy system, which everyone who has never tried swears by, and scrub our bottom every six or eight weeks. It was for that purpose that one of the first places we visited when we returned 'home' was Roundwood Quay. It's an historic quay owned by the National Trust, beautifully built from drystone, grassed on top, and drying about 200 metres beyond the low-water mark. It's not every boater's cup of tea – although the River Fal is one of the busiest pleasure-boating estuaries in Britain, Roundwood Quay is almost unvisited from seaward. It's nerve-racking to bring an unblemished white hull within a few inches of a drystone wall, and in any case, 'drying out' is taboo with most owners of fin-keeled boats – which accounts for about 95 per cent of *all* boats. So we get Roundwood to ourselves. We tie a line to a granite bollard, and a second one to the granite leg of a seat erected by the National Trust – there is another bollard but it's a long way away, and not in a useful place – then we tie the mast to the trunk of an oak tree so that our boat doesn't fall over when the water's gone out.

Granite post

Waiting for the tide to go out gives us a chance to stretch our legs, and to try to piece together the purpose of all the earthworks on the hill above the quay, dating from the Industrial Revolution, and back in history to the Iron Age trenches of a fort.

When our imaginations had taken us as far as they could go with all that, Linda cut my hair. We sat on the bench ashore to avoid getting hair trimmings on board, and hoped that no walkers would arrive and catch us during our odd behaviour. I don't think I've ever had such a scenic haircut. We heard the voices of walkers, and a moment later they appeared from around a bush. We wondered what they would make of it – would they skirt around us, walk the other way, pretend not to see us? No: one of them sat quietly down beside me.

'I'm next,' he said.

For the following two or three hours we were industrious, scrubbing the hull with nylon scouring pads, jollying ourselves along by arguing about whose side was worst and had the greatest workload, whilst we raced against time and tide to get the job done. Just in the nick, as the tide began to return, we climbed back up the old stone steps – thoughtfully built so that they tilted into the quay, and if you slipped, you slipped the right way – with our bowls and our pads, and our faces splashed algae green, but our work complete.

Late in the afternoon a woman in her 70s wandered onto the quay in a light summer dress and sat down on the bench to which we were tied. There were three or four houses forming a tiny hamlet close by and it seemed to us she had come from one of them. She began a conversation which went on for an hour or more, roaming all kinds of subjects, but returning often to the theme of her husband, now deceased, and his love of boats and sailing. Jean – as we came to learn she was called – spoke nostalgically of places far away visited under sail and of returns to this very quay, where her husband would tie up as we were tied up now. We wondered, naturally enough, if she glimpsed in us her and her husband's 'younger selves'. At last she got up to leave, and speaking in that candid way in which we all wish we could speak – but which seems to be the privilege of the elderly – told us it had been lovely to relive pleasant memories through us. Not only had we enjoyed her company but, confidentially, we had wondered at first if she had come to tell us off for tying up to a National Trust bench.

As she left to walk home, she turned. 'And I know that Wally would be honoured to have such a pretty boat tied to his bench.'

When she'd gone I examined the bench. Discreetly fastened at the back, out of view, was a memorial plaque dedicated to the memory of Walter McKay 1919–1999.

The following day found us anchored a few hundred yards away, opposite *Smuggler's Cottage*, where the American flag still flies in honour of the troops stationed there during World War II and commemorates the fact that General Eisenhower, Supreme Commander of Allied Forces in Europe, visited the cottage to address his troops prior to their embarkation for the D-Day landings.

On our shore were the retired wrecks of two fishing boats, which leant into each other for support like a couple of drunks, and no longer rose with the tide. A harbour authority notice, typed on A4 paper and slipped inside a clear plastic wallet, condensation causing the ink to run, was tacked to one of them, putting its unknown owner on notice that the authority intended to remove the vessel and break it up unless he claimed it within three months. No one came forward.

This vessel will be broken up if unclaimed

From here we walked along a footpath – seldom trod – to a place we love. Neither one of us can put into words what it is about the popping low-water ooze of Cowlands Creek, or its scattering of stone cottages, that draws us back and back. Its boats are beached high up the shore, awaiting work, and are all in the traditional style of the area – the Quay Punt – and those boats which are not actually built of wood *seem* to be, lending the place a timeless, forgotten air. By way of emphasis, on the opposite shore there is a modest stone quay, backed by a tumbledown shed, overgrown with trees whose branches bend down almost to the water, and have absorbed the handful of boats which are tied bows-on, by rotting cordage. Two of the boats are yachts with tattered sails – blown out in some unremembered gale – hanging in rags from algae-green masts. The quay, the mooring lines and the boats, too, are the same powder green, looking like a film set built 50 years ago, and then not required.

We found the creek by accident long before we lived on board a boat. Soon after Linda and I met, we'd come down to Cornwall with a tent along a road which had taken so many unlikely turns that we couldn't rightly say *where* we were, and only stepped out of the car because the road had come to a dead end at the water's edge. To our right, an elderly man was in his garden, weeding. We called 'hello' and asked if he could give us directions to the nearest campsite. He thought for a long while.

'I can't say there *is* one,' he said. 'Not for miles. But, look 'ere, if you don't mind goats, why not pitch your tent in my garden?'

It felt as though several birthdays had just come at once.

'Here's a good spot,' he said. 'See how the grass is long? That'll be lovely and soft, that will... and in the morning you'll have eggs – if my hens are behaving. Are you all right for water? Here he is now – look! The honey-coloured one there with the horns and the long beard – he's the one to watch... But I'll be putting them in later. You won't have to worry then.'

That night was the highlight of our camping holiday.

Twelve years later we stumbled upon the place again by chance, soon after we'd launched the boat and were living on board; at that time we learned from someone that the name of the man who'd lent us his garden was Gunn. Today, when we walked into the hamlet there he was, outside his house and working on a boat. We wondered if he'd remember us.

Perhaps he did. At least, he pretended to, and sat on the hull of an up-turned boat to make our acquaintance anew. He was as unhurried and as open-hearted as we remembered him. After a few minutes his wife joined us, cast a blank look over us, and said nothing. She sat so close beside her husband that they were touching. He raised a shaggy brow in her direction, paused there long enough to learn something about her, then he was back with us.

'Were you *born* in your house?' I asked.

'No,' he said, seeming only too aware of how quaint my question made him sound. He tossed his head toward the neighbouring house. 'I was born in that one.'

His wife held up her hand in front of us. It had three fingers and a stub where the fourth should be. 'See that finger?' She smiled. 'I lost it in a chaff-cutter when I was a little girl of six. I ran indoors screaming. My mum, when she saw it, she says: "Ooooh!"'

Mrs Gunn was a good actress, and played her mother's part, grasping her young hand into her own, drawing a sharp intake of breath, and flashing her eyes, warning of a greater significance to the accident than was apparent. She paused for effect, eyes wide as saucers.

'That's your ring finger!' she whispered.

When she'd finished, Mr Gunn continued with what he'd been saying. A minute later when he'd finished, his wife spoke again.

'My friends were all jealous when Victor asked me to marry him – he was such a catch... they were all after him!' She giggled.

'They don't want to hear all that...' Mr Gunn protested, bashfully, and then opened up a new conversation, telling us about oyster fishing, and about his own work. Mrs Gunn sat in silence for a while, hands folded on her lap – she seemed to drift away for a while, but when there was another pause in the conversation, she looked up to see if this was her opportunity, then spoke again.

'See that finger? I lost that in a chaff-cutter when I was a little girl of six...'

Catching our eye, Mr Gunn mouthed something to us.
Noticing that, his wife turned to him. 'Eh?'
He shook his head.
His wife dried up. They sat staring, each at their feet.

* * *

We'd been invited to a party further along the coast at Fowey
to celebrate the completion of a stylish cabin-next-the-water,
having been converted from an old pilchard-curing shed. The
guys throwing the party owned a newly-built pilot cutter to
which we'd lost a race by rather a long margin. But that didn't
stop us dreaming that we might somehow win the next. Their
boat was built by Luke Powell of Working Sail, who builds to
an old recipe, using massive timbers, sweetly curved. Each is
a sight for sore eyes. The pilchard shed sat on its own quay,
allowing them to moor their boat outside their front door,
and they'd invited us – together with a few other classic-boat
owners – to tie up alongside, step ashore, and enjoy the fun.
What could be more convenient for folk who live aboard?
The party wasn't for a month but we set off now because you
do when you've got the whole summer to yourself, and half a
reason to make a journey.

The river was in full-summer swing when we left it: life
was teeming – every rising tide brought leaps and splashes
with the creeping water-edge. A cormorant surfaced with
a young pollack in his beak, unable to believe his luck.
The fuss he made as he tried to swallow it attracted the
attention of a black-backed gull, which crashed on top of the
cormorant in a failed attempt to steal it. The cormorant was
too quick, and dived with his fish, popping up again a few
seconds later. The gull was back, the cormorant dived – the
battle went on for two or three minutes until the cormorant,
forced to spend longer and longer underwater and out of
breath, gave up, allowing the black-backed gull to take
his fish.

These scenes we left behind for the more barren but freer
seas, setting out on one of those days when short waves rolled
into the river, shortened by the shoaling water, lifting our bow

and dropping it heavily into the trough which followed. Not without misgivings did we leave the tranquillity of the river behind, and ask ourselves if this was the best day on which to travel, seeing as we could choose any.

On the radio someone called the Coastguard in an urgent voice, without identifying himself. The Coastguard answered.

'There are dolphins in the harbour!' said the voice.

'Are they in any danger?' There was something sobering about the Coastguard's tone.

'No...' said the caller. He couldn't think what came next, and un-keyed his microphone.

Dolphins have that effect on we humans – but I'm glad it wasn't me that made the call.

At sea we put the waves onto our starboard beam and headed out for deeper water where they lengthened until we scarcely noticed them. It was a fine day for a sail, after all.

We rolled ahead, pushing white foam with our bow, tied the tiller just off to windward, and let our boat steer herself over the waves whilst the singing bubbles of our bow wave streamed out astern. Journeys like this cost nothing and reward us much – the air smells fresh and healthy, and life seems full of purpose. Two hours later we rounded Dodman Point and swung into the north, slowly turning back on ourselves into the west toward Mevagissey Harbour, our first stop. It was also our first ever visit to that port and we scarcely knew what to expect. Well, that's not quite true – we'd been there as tourists a couple of times and eaten fish and chips overlooking the inner harbour, but we'd never arrived by boat. I thought how lovely it would be to make our entrance under sail, the wind being fair, but baulked at the last minute. On paper it lends itself to that plan, but perhaps the harbour master there wouldn't approve of that sort of behaviour in his port? And what if we sailed in and found no time to shorten sail, ran into the north arm and carried away its beacon? Visiting yachts lie alongside the outer wall, moored to rings which, at low water, might be twenty feet above their heads. It was low water now. How would we get a line ashore without a 'boy' to catch it?

Rolling over a lazy sea

So we rounded up into wind on the *outside* of the harbour wall, to the intense irritation of a score of fishermen whose lines we could see glittering like spiders' threads in the sunlight ahead of us. At first they stood glumly next to their rods, staring in abject boredom into the apparently lifeless water before them, then started throwing us grudgingly admiring looks – coming as we did to relieve their monotony – then there were stirrings of action, murmurs of irritation that we might frighten the fish, and finally, the most animated scene imaginable, when it became clear that we intended to sail through the nylon arch they had formed. They leapt to snatch up their rods and wind in their lines, beginning with the man nearest followed be each in turn down the quay wall in a spasm of activity as they raced to save their gear. I called up my apologies but there was no reply because there'd been no time to appoint a spokesperson to receive my apology on all their behalves. We fired up the engine, circled round for the entrance, and left them in a cloud of black smoke.

Inside, we tied alongside the harbour wall with the help of a holidaymaker who was on top of it, and who had made the mistake of looking over the wall just when we wanted someone. With one line ashore I raced up a ladder that was set into the stone wall – buried amongst the wet seaweed – with the second rope between my teeth. There was an old wooden boat tied ahead of us and we fell into conversation with them. Their lives echoed our own exactly. Conversation turned to where they would live along the south coast if they were to live in a house. They were all for Dittisham, a village on the banks of the River Dart, and since it enjoys some of the highest property prices in the region, and money was the thing in shortest supply for both of us, we recognised them to be hopeless dreamers... and got on like a house afire.

Next stop was Newton Ferrers, just east of Plymouth. We'd made the mistake once of tying alongside the pontoon in the River Yealm. Not this time. We were no worse off lying to our own anchor a kilometre down river at Cellar Bay. No worse off? Better off by almost thirty quid! That's almost two pints of ale at The Swan. For complete comfort in Cellar Bay it helps if the wind has either died to nothing, or doesn't have much west in it.

We've never been into Salcombe, which lay next along our course. My gran was born in Salcombe a hundred years ago – she's dead now, of course – but I'd quite like to see the place. Visiting yachtsmen wishing to lie to their own anchor in Salcombe Harbour are welcome to try their luck near the entrance in an area noted for its poor holding and swell. For this the harbour authority halve their normal charges, reducing the fee to about double what you'd expect to pay for a *pontoon* berth anywhere else. If the yachtsman actually wishes to come *in*, picking up a mooring is compulsory. The moorings are overlooked by 20,000 people. They bounce around to the wash of 100 cruisers rushing home to their wardened accommodation in time for a sundowner, and mooring fees are higher than anywhere else in Europe, with the possible exception of Monaco. We thumb our nose at Salcombe when we pass – though I'd still like to visit one day, perhaps by coach, when I retire. I wonder if anyone offers retirement coach-trips to Salcombe?

So we pressed on for Dartmouth even though there wasn't a breath of wind, the tide had turned against us, and it was beginning to look as though we might not get there for a month. Evening arrived, and the number of sails on the water grew fewer and fewer. A telegraph pole which broke the horizon in the west became compellingly interesting to us, being the only thing going on in our lives just then. We played the parlour-game of guessing what it was: an oil rig, the mast for a wind turbine being manoeuvred, or was it actually... a telegraph pole? Linda got it right: she said it would turn out to be a tall ship, and so it did. It took more than two hours for the tall ship to climb up over the curve of the globe behind us, parade itself, and then to slide downhill toward the east, and in all that time we covered just three of the seven miles from Start Point to the entrance of the Dart. By the time we made the entrance it was dark and we were both dazzled and dizzied by the lights of the town, and by the merry criss-crossings of ferries – confident of their right-of-way – cutting across our bow with four inches to spare or passing astern in carefully planned near-misses, as much as to say: *You're new here, aren't you?*

We found our way to the main anchorage, which looked busy, but motoring through it, discovered a hole just the right size. A huge schooner was our nearest neighbour. As we passed under its stern we brushed the lifeless folds of an American flag the size of a stage curtain on Broadway, washed and ironed and suspended from what looked like a varnished tree overhanging the vessel's stern. Our anchor chain rattled into the deep water alongside the schooner, and every time I glanced that way I was met with twinkles of light reflected in the varnished cherry posts of its deck railings. Having nothing to be ashamed of ourselves, we felt positively scruffy.

Our anchor was followed by a carefully measured scope of chain so that we couldn't interfere with the schooner, or anyone else – a few turns of chain round the Samson post, and the day's work was done.

I was just walking back to the cockpit when I heard a voice call out in the dark: 'Say! D'ya think that's gonna fly?'

Because the accent was American, and had that 'friendly stranger at the bar' quality, I guessed it must be coming from the schooner and belonged to its owner. I scanned the boat's length until my eye met with the well-fed figure of a man, amidships, leaning over the rail in silhouette, casually arranged with one foot resting on the stringer – just as you see passengers who are 'frequent cruisers' arrange themselves when their liner is in port. Next I had to work out *what* he was asking me 'might fly', and my first thought was that we'd arrived at Dartmouth during one of those amateur air-shows when people strap a pair of patio doors to their back and peddle off the end of a pier. Because I'm not a film-goer and don't own a television I've never learned the language, so it took a few moments for the penny to drop that he was questioning the legitimacy of my anchoring decision.

'Oh!' I said, matching his friendly tone. 'You mean do I think this will *work*? Yes, it'll be just fine.'

To my surprise, my words and manner touched his fuse. After a pause during which it smouldered, he roared like a cannon, and his words echoed back to us from around the harbour: 'WOSSA MADDA WITH YOU GUYS? YOU'RE THE SECOND FELLA TO ANCHOR TOO CLOSE... SAY, THERE'S PLENNYA ROOM OVER THERE...' He pointed.

'Please don't worry – we'll be OK here,' I assured him.

'BUT, WHY DONCHA JUSS PICK YA ANCHOR UP AND DROP IT OVER THERE – LOOK AT ALL THE ROOM YA GETTING... AND YA'LL HAVE ALL TO YOURSELF!'

His wife sat like an unsold doll inside the glass cabinet of their dining room, grimly forbearing under a beehive of hair as she watched the soufflé in her dish collapse.

'CAN YOU SEE ALL THAT SPACE YA GETT'N..?'

'That's *very* thoughtful of you – but we're happy here,' I told him in the tone English people use when we want to antagonise our American cousins. 'Anyway, it's been lovely chatting to you,' I continued, infuriatingly, 'but I'm afraid I've got to go because my dinner is ready.' Then I slipped below into the yellow light of our saloon.

'Have you been upsetting our neighbours?' Linda asked.

The tide was due to turn in about an hour, which could bring about the chaos the schooner envisaged.

After dinner Linda said, 'Are we going to move?'

'Of course not!'

'Right then, I'm off to bed.'

After washing up I turned out the cabin lights and peeped into the darkness toward the schooner, and saw the black shape of the owner against the backdrop of the town's lights, holding a lonely vigil on the bridge, awaiting the turn of the tide. I slipped into the cockpit, dressed in dark colours, and hitched the tiller over to port so that the ebb would stretch our chain away from the schooner. A quarter of an hour later the gap between us had grown, so I went to bed.

On the sunny morning which followed we began by motoring the short distance to the fishing pontoons, found a gap, and filled our freshwater tank. Then, before heading upriver to explore with the new tide, I had the childish whim to motor back through the anchored vessels and wish seven of the eight vessels there a 'Good morning!' Everyone seemed to be in the cockpit of their boats at breakfast and sang out a cheerful reply as we passed. The schooners sat stiffly on their poop-deck, occasionally brushing crumbs of croissant from the linen fastened in the American-style about their necks. They looked up, wearing half-smiles, when it seemed we would come their way, but they were too immaculately dressed to go splashing them with the milk of human kindness. We passed them by without glancing in their direction. Even Linda played along, and she won't normally sink that low.

Sailing up the Dart is full of interest: whereas Dartmouth and Kingswear – the towns on either side of the river near its entrance – are terraced on steep hills overlooking the water, the land upriver quickly becomes low-lying and pastoral. The land being flatter, the breeze returned with enough strength to fill our canvas, allowing us to sail silently past woodlands, Devonshire hedged-fields, parklands which rolled up to historic houses set amid farm estates, and thatched 'fisherman's' cottages sitting at the water's edge, fronted by cobbled slipways, unchanged in hundreds of years. As we drifted by, the sounds of water birds trilling were our musical accompaniment.

The river took us on its meandering course up to Bow Creek, where I was hoping to slip into the Maltster's Arms at Tuckenhay for a beer, but I misjudged the entrance to the creek. I didn't run aground, unusually for me, but there was less water at the entrance than I had been expecting. Wading birds were standing alongside us, and they were only up to their knees. Nor could I find the channel. The 'chart' we were using was printed on the back of a tourist guide for the area, and competed for space with advertisements. It was marked *Not to be used for navigation*, but it had done rather well up until then. We backtracked a few hundred yards and threw our anchor out under the branches of a tree into such a shallow part of the river that I swear I could see one of its flukes sticking up at low water.

The following day we went for a walk past where Carpenter Oak have their workshops. They're joiners who build those houses which echo medieval halls and have their frames, and the structure of the roof, on display from the inside. It was a Sunday. I didn't want to pass by on a workday in case I alarmed them by staring mournfully in at them over the hedge. I want an oak-framed house, one day. I mean, I *really* want one. For ten minutes I savoured the sweet smell of fresh-cut green oak, and wondered if I would ever be walking into their yard as a bona-fide customer.

We caught the afternoon tide back down to Dittisham, and the Ferry Boat Inn, run by a gay couple. I know, I know, that sounds like a homophobic remark, but isn't intended to be – gay people make better hosts and *intend* you to have a great night out. That evening the Ferry Boat Inn was noisy with customers brimming with good cheer.

A man made his way through the crowd toward us and introduced himself as Paul. 'Is that your boat... the green one?' he said.

'It is – yes.'

Paul was so effusive in his praise, so interested in our story, that we invited him to join us on the next leg of our journey to Plymouth.

We picked him up at six in the morning a day or two later from the quay at Greenaway, before the ferry started work, and got out on the last of the ebb. Showing off, *Caol Ila* sailed like a dream. The day was spent tacking into head winds and rip tides, struggling to get back round Start Point. Looking along the deck to where our bowsprit pointed on each new tack gave hope, but the tidal stream pushed us back and stole our advantage, allowing us to gain only a few yards – every time we closed with the land we saw the same rocks, only from a slightly different angle. Linda and I would bemoan such slow progress, but having someone new on board, and someone who was having a lovely time at that, made us keep our mouths shut.

By early evening we'd got ourselves well inside Plymouth Sound, past the breakwater, and were just deciding where to park up when we discovered that the engine wouldn't start. Fortunately our guest knew Plymouth Harbour quite well and suggested that in the circumstances we should go to the Mayflower Marina because they've got the longest outer pontoon you've ever seen, and it would be easy to sail onto.

He was right. Even the naval operations which had closed the water through which we wanted to sail for most of the afternoon opened again just as we arrived. And because there were no other boats on the pontoon, we had about three hundred yards to aim at. Even we managed that.

Things were a bit of a mess down below after our passage – wet oilies, dirty cups, wet cabin sole – and because everyone was tired there was no enthusiasm for cooking. Paul offered to take us for a pub meal. Walking the streets of Plymouth after dark is probably all right if you know what you're about, but what with litter blowing through empty streets, and metal-shuttered doors covered with graffiti tags, it felt slimy. Perhaps we weren't in the best bit.

We found a pub whose menu board, chained down in the street outside, was so spattered with exclamation marks as to leave you in no doubt about the landlord's enthusiasm for the food he was offering. That, or there were a lot of seagulls in the area. We walked in to receive a sincere and cheerful greeting from the landlord, who stood behind a Wild West-styled bar which had seen a good deal of action. He was chummy, stubbly, and had exactly the sort of muscular physique you'd need to maintain law and order, and not only that, but something about his welcome reassured us that he'd take our side if anything kicked off.

Tattooed customers, quiet as nuns, lined the bar in front of pints. There was a smell of stale beer, and the carpet felt crisp underfoot.

'You eatin'?' the landlord called as we took our seats.

'Yes please.'

'Ere ya, then,' he said as he rushed round from the bar. 'Don't sit there – come into the lounge.' And with that he ushered us from the fuggy warmth of the saloon bar into a cold and empty room: poorly lit, linoleum floors, with no windows and lots of tables draped with gingham cloths. Salt, pepper, vinegar and brown sauce were already thoughtfully in place.

We chose Sirloin Steak with 'Provincial' Sauce, which turned out to be a piece of leather floating in a tin of ratatouille under a white-pepper crust. None of us spoke, nor could we speak. Those steaks had been exercising our jaws for twenty minutes when to our surprise the kitchen door burst open and a man rushed at us dressed as a convict, fire flashing in his eyes.

'Ows ya steak?' he asked, and darted enquiring glances at each of us, causing his earrings to bang against his tattooed neck.

'Absolutely lovely!' we said, united in terror.

'What about the sauce?'

'Perfect!'

'Made that meself!'

'Did you?'

'Yeah! Go on – I'll get you some more!' And with that he disappeared, reappearing moments later with an industrial-sized saucepan, the contents of which he glooped onto our plates with the look of a man who knew that he was spreading gastronomic happiness.

Returning to the boat late at night we found we were still the only craft moored to the 300-metre pontoon, and threw nervous glances around to know the reason for it. At 2am the boat was thrown onto the pontoon, sliding off again moments later. A swell had got up which mostly just banged us against the pontoon so hard it deflated the fenders, but every twenty minutes we'd be carried bodily onto the pontoon, left high and dry for a moment, then fall back with a splash. It was anyone's guess which would break first – the floating pontoon, or our hull. We stumbled away in different directions, dazed and wondering how this place could conceivably be called a 'harbour', to look for more substantial fenders, and found some lorry tyres someone had thoughtfully left for the next boat to make the mistake of mooring here. It seemed to me that there ought to be a notice up, warning people that this sort of thing occurred just here, as I told the marina manager the following morning. He sat and listened to me, wearing the thin lipped smile you expect from a man who harboured boats, and secrets. Paul left us to our salty life the following morning, life aboard having palled.

We set off for Fowey on one of those perfect Cornish coast days. The swell had disappeared as mysteriously as it had arrived, leaving a ruffled blue sea, flashing occasionally with a white-capped wave. A soft wind blew from the land allowing us to parade our sail close to the shoreline and admire the view: past Looe Island, long-time home and idyllic retreat of the Atkins sisters; Udder Rock, idyllic retreat of dogfish; and then began to beat upwind into Fowey. It isn't often that we come out on top compared with the boats going our way, but as luck would have it we chanced upon a slant of wind which carried us straight into the harbour on a single-tack, leaving a handful of other craft stitching back and forth outside, who could only gaze after us in wonder.

Amongst the trees we saw the pilchard shed, and just off the shore, a gathering of boats for the party. There was nearly an embarrassing accident yards from the quay when a chap who was on the phone, and looking dead ahead as he sat on the flying bridge of his motor cruiser, reversed across our bow. I whistled a warning. Fortunately he had quite big engines, there was a puff of smoke, and his boat was gone. We tied up.

Hesper's *bowsprit*

Hesper – a 44ft Scillies Pilot Cutter – was holding a kind of open day. We poked around on board to admire the accommodation and the powerful deck gear that had allowed them to overtake us when we'd been sailing along at an unprecedented 11.2 knots with all plain sail hoisted, and a gale of wind behind us. Exploring with us were another couple who seemed very knowledgeable about her 'type', and were examining her in forensic detail.

Back on deck I said, 'We'll really have our work cut out to beat her!'

'Which boat is yours?' the woman asked, blinking.

'That's us,' I said, pointing to our boat, tied alongside. It looked pathetically small all of a sudden.

'Well, you won't beat her with *that!*' she scoffed.

Men are quite fragile things – you can rob them, cheat them, and lie to them, but you can't insult either their car or their boat without crushing them.

She spoke over my wounded silence: 'We'd have our work cut out beating her in *our* boat, and she wins more trophies than we've got cabinets for.'

'Which boat is yours?' I asked.

She pointed to a sleek-looking Bristol Channel Pilot Cutter – long, low, and as thin as a racing-snake.

Bristol Channel Pilot Cutters are the racehorses of the classic boat world. The age of sail came to an end round about the close of the 1800s, as boats began to get reliable engines put in them. Up until then the world's cargo was moved from continent to continent under shaking canvas by tall-masted vessels which, arriving near their destination, would employ the services of a 'pilot' – a man so familiar with the local waters that the incoming vessel and its valuable cargo could be placed in his care. The rule amongst pilots – who competed for work by sailing out over the empty horizon and looking for incoming sail – was that the first pilot to board the tall ship got the work. Because of this pilot cutters – the boats in which pilots sailed – were constantly being improved in their design. Each new pilot cutter came off the stocks incorporating some improvement on what had been learned already, over generations, experience being passed down from father to son. The racing snake was obviously such a boat.

Many of the partygoers were staying on for a day, but we left early the next morning before any of the bears were up with their sore heads. We slipped away so as not to disturb anyone, hoisted full canvas on the mirrored water of the river, turned toward the mouth and felt the press of a soft breeze, just strong enough to straighten out the folds in our sails and no more. From the mouth of the harbour, vessels heading west need to clear a navigational buoy – marking rocks and shoals – at a distance of two miles. With the wind fine on our port bow it looked very much as though – if we concentrated – we would just squeak through on one course, so I settled down happily to that work, following the wind's every flaw. Linda appeared in the hatchway with a steaming mug of tea. Something over my shoulder caught her eye. She did a double-take.

'Don't look now... but there's a Bristol Channel Pilot Cutter following you.'

My jaw fell.

'Who is it?'

'That boat from yesterday...'

The racing snake was coming for us. I didn't even dare to turn.

'How far away?'

'Ooh... four hundred yards?'

'Motoring or sailing?'

'Just getting the last of her sails up now...'

I decided I wouldn't look behind at all, I'd just concentrate on what I was doing. That way I wouldn't be tempted to sail too close to the wind, our boat would make her best speed, and we would delay for as long as possible the moment at which the Racing Snake overtook us.

Caol Ila stepped over the water, never lost the lightly-pressing wind in her sails, and nosed her course over the slight swell quietly and efficiently, without wasting energy by making foam.

I exhausted Linda by asking how we were doing every two minutes, taking heart from her non-committal answers, which always ended with '...looks about the same to me.'

My heart was pounding; muscles tense, it was hard to breathe, my palms were sweaty and every nerve tingled as I watched the wind and the water. Turning around the buoy we could ease our course a few degrees, the sails settled more decidedly, and our speed notched up a couple of 'tenths', freezing the digits at just under three knots.

Linda announced that she was going to have her 'bath', leaving me without a report for half an hour – but still I daren't turn round.

When she came back up I was desperate to hear how we were doing. All I knew was that they hadn't overtaken us, and I could scarcely believe *that*.

In answer to my inevitable question Linda made humming and err-ing noises before concluding: 'Well, if anything, we've pulled slightly ahead.'

'What?!' I wanted to shout. 'Ahead!'

For three draining hours we sailed on. During the last hour we secured a lead it would be hard to throw away. Shortly after that, with eight miles still to home, the Bristol Channel Pilot Cutter drew alongside within hailing distance, sails down, engine hammering – it was my first glimpse of her.

The skipper cupped his hands to speak. 'She goes nicely!' he called.

'Oh – thanks!' I said, hoping my voice wouldn't give me away.

'We've got to get back,' he said, 'so we're going to motor on.'

With a wave of farewell he ploughed a furrow toward Falmouth, rising and falling on the long swell.

'What a nice chap...' I said to Linda when they'd gone. 'I would have been far too stingy to make that acknowledgement if the situation had been reversed.'

Something compelled me to carry on 'going nicely', even when the wind fell light. Seven hours later we entered the harbour, bristling with pride.

Sailing up the Fal

12 WOMAN OVERBOARD

BOILING HALF A GALLON OF VINEGAR FOR FOUR HOURS in the confines of our small boat runs the risk of killing the woodworm, so when we want to make chutney with autumn fruits we've gathered on our long walks we do it over a camp fire on the beach. We'd got two bags of wild plums and thought we might kill two birds with one stone by making our chutney up the Percuil River. Although the Percuil is choked with moorings – lots of boats take advantage of the protection offered by the twists and turns of the river. Where it branches in three separate directions at once there's a silted area which virtually dries on low spring tides, and so is clear of moorings. At neaps, when the tide neither rises high nor falls low, there's plenty of room and water for visitors to anchor.

The other advantage of boiling up our chutney hereabouts is that the village of St Mawes, which lies at the entrance to the Percuil, has the Waterside Gallery, which sells some of my maritime artwork. So we took the opportunity of dropping off some artwork to James, who owns the gallery. He says it adds a touch of romance to the 'story' of the drawings that they have arrived by boat, under sail, virtually to the gallery's front door. I, on the other hand, feel a complete fraud doing that because I was brought up with the idea that working isn't supposed to be fun.

After tea and a chat with James we continued up the Percuil. There's a channel between the moorings, apparently,

Careened for cleaning – we pull her off balance whilst there is still enough water around her to give her a soft landing (page 6).

Above A good boat in a seaway – broad in the beam.

Below left Scotland is all rocks; rocks to protect our boat and ...

Below right ... rocks to lean against – Justin and Linda.

Above The beautiful Loch Tarbert (page 6).

Below With the nose of our bowsprit in a holly bush, Cornwall.

Above left *Caol Ila*, the boat,
parked outside
Caol Ila, the distillery.

Above right The cosy harbour
at Strangford.

Right What's going on in there?
Scooter, our new salty sea
dog.

Above 'Just then I saw a flash go off from the end of the pier' (page 63).

Below The awful shore where the *Exmouth* went down (page 13).

Above 'We slipped through a naturally-formed canal' (page 3).

Below left Scotland is noted for the colours of her landscape.

Below right The mast tied to a tree at Roundwood Quay (page 112).

Above A dreach morning over Texa, the Inner Hebrides.

Below left There are 8,000 red deer on Jura, and just 200 people.

Below right Living aboard, we still get nosy neighbours.

A proper water bed.

but we've never found it. We aimed between pairs of boats and tried to time our passage so that as they swung to their moorings, the space between them was big enough for us to get through. We dropped anchor on the silted flats a short distance away from another live-aboard, who we only saw from time to time. He kept very much to himself, though we'd met him once. He was affable, diffident, modest and smiling. He lived on his boat so that his daughter and her child could live in his house. Where he went during the long months when we didn't see him, we never knew – he must know out-of-the-way spots which we have yet to discover.

Sitting on a beach overhung with trees, next to a fire, stirring a cauldron of chutney for three hours is one of the most purposeful and fulfilling jobs life has to offer. I was in heaven. If people would pay me to do it, I'd build myself a hut and never leave that beach. And a bonus is that you end up with a dozen or fifteen jars of relish for the trifling cost of the vinegar. Each of the jars we make is authenticated as genuine by the little black fragments of charcoal suspended in the liquor. Try as you might, you can't *buy* anything like that anywhere in the world.

'Justin? I don't know if you've heard but there's a storm coming.' John was on the phone. We *had* heard that it was going to be blowy the following day, but just at present it was so lovely we couldn't really believe it, and hadn't taken much notice.

'Get yourself really well dug-in because it's going to be a bad one,' he said.

The wind was forecast to be Storm Force 10. Even then we weren't too bothered because we were in the best spot – our anchor was set in thick black mud and because it was so shallow a 'sea' couldn't really build over it, not even in a storm.

But John's words pricked my conscience. We stripped the foresails off the boat and dropped the boom to the deck. We would have settled for that if we hadn't spotted our neighbour setting a second anchor. So we veered a second anchor at 'open hawse', as the expression is when two anchors and their chain form a 'V' shape ahead of you. There really was nothing more that we could do.

When the storm hit it turned out to be one of those dry gales of wind which shriek through the rigging blowing a steady note, rather than the more turbulent squall-and-lull kind of storms which are interspersed by periods of torrential rain. It was like being in a wind tunnel. The first casualty we saw was an eight-seater inflatable dinghy parting company from its mooring and cartwheeling over the water as it came upriver towards us. Sometimes it flew up like a kite, only to crash into the water like a shot bird, then began cartwheeling once again. Eventually it reached the shore where it caught in the branches of a tree. Moments later another inflatable followed it, then a third, so that we wondered if every inflatable in the river would come up one by one. Next came two mooring buoys with a chugging motion, dragging their chains along the bottom behind them. They heaved past us on the swell, which was bigger than we had expected, racing each other to the shore.

Every wave to pass us was breaking, and threw itself with a slap at the sides of our hull as we weaved, riding to our port anchor, then our starboard.

A couple of yachts broke free from their moorings. The first clouted the boat behind to leave it shuddering with the impact, delivering glancing blows to everything else it hit. We followed it with our eyes, ready to fend off if it came toward us, but it passed wide. The second was charmed and ran the gauntlet without a strike. By teatime the wind had fallen to an ordinary gale; it had shaken everything loose that was *coming* loose, and, by dinner time, the air was still and the water calm. The following day we re-rigged for sunny weather.

We motored past our neighbour, who came up from below decks, smiled, and called something out to us which we didn't hear. So we nodded, and shouted 'Yes!' like you do. We can't hear anything when our engine is running.

Our engine – a Perkins P4 – was built sixty years ago, weighs half a ton, leaks oil, and sounds like it's drilling a mineshaft through granite. The normal way of acquiring a marine engine is 'incidentally' – one will be bolted on somewhere when you buy your boat. Most folk don't even know where their engine is. After all, it's not like boats have a bonnet or anything. Virtually silent in operation, the only time you ever notice an engine on most boats is when they don't work, because the engine box has been super-lined with sound-proofing. When we were building our engine box, one look at the price of 'marine' soundproofing sheets outraged me, so I fell victim, once again, to my own meanness and we'd never installed any. In another year or two both Linda and I will be stone deaf.

On the way back to Falmouth from Ireland a couple of years earlier I was so tired, with only 12 miles to go, that I went down below, intending to shut my eyes for a few minutes, and lay down with my head resting against the throbbing engine box. The vibration turned my brain to butter because the next thing I knew, I heard an urgent voice calling and opened my eyes to see a stranger standing before me, apparently in distress. I struggled to my feet and followed her up some stairs, which led outside. When the fresh air hit me, I was surprised to discover that I was on a boat and at sea, and stood there trying to take it all in. It dawned on me then that not only did I not know who the woman was, I didn't know who *I* was either, and sat down in calm silence. There are frustrations in the complex lives of every adult – yet for five or ten glorious minutes I was as a child, without a concern in the world, utterly free to enjoy the breeze in my hair and the sun in my eyes. Even so, I had no regrets when my memory began to return. I didn't mention it to Linda, who only thought I was behaving 'oddly'; she would have been hurt that I couldn't remember who she was, worried that I couldn't remember why we were on a boat, and annoyed that I didn't know what we were supposed to be doing next.

It was time to do something about that engine box – though I felt a bit of a fraud standing in the queue of the carpet department. All the other customers were there legitimately, and if any of them were queuing for underlay, it was to go under a carpet – but *I* wanted some underlay for an engine box. I knew they'd be suspicious. I mean, three metres isn't even enough for a lavatory, but I was embarrassed to tell them what it was *really* for. The shop I was in was a chain of retail outlets in the south west whose terms and conditions of employment are so appalling that the staff they *do* get aren't – you know... they're not the sharpest tools in the box. Don't get me wrong, they're all lovely and that, but when you take your custom into a shop you like to be valued as a customer, made to feel as though you *are* someone. They don't do that there. They won't lie to you. What you get is rock-bottom prices – take it or leave it. The first thing you notice as you pass down the aisles of tat intermingled with stuff that really is top-notch is that they operate one of those old-fashioned loudspeaker systems so that 'office' can speak to 'staff' without having to go and look for them. But some of the messages are so intimate you wonder if they've noticed that they've got a shop full of customers: 'Will someone go to DIY? There's a customer waiting... and that's the third time I've had to ask! Oh, and by the way, Tammy... the hospital's just phoned – your dad's died.'

Standing in the queue of the carpet department I rehearsed what I was going to say. The blokes behind the counter dismissed the people in front of me one by one, empty-handed – a lot of people, it seems, had joined the queue without sufficient information to make a purchase. I didn't want to leave empty-handed, but they operated a zero-tolerance regime for time-wasters. Of the two chaps behind the counter, I particularly hoped I wouldn't get one. You know how we've all got about 2.5 per cent Neanderthal DNA in us – well, what they don't tell you is that that's only an *average* for *all* of us. Some people have got more than their fair share. The bloke I didn't want to be served by looked as though he'd won the Neanderthal DNA lottery, and had fur growing on his forehead. Five minutes later I was face to face with him. Looking into his eyes I felt I could see all eternity.

'Hello!' I said cheerfully.

He waited, to see what I would do next.

'Could I have 3 square metres of underlay?'

The rolls, it transpired, were 1.2 metres wide which threw up the immediate problem of where to cut it to produce a piece of 3 square metres.

'We don't do it like that...' he told me. 'You have to tell me the size of your room, then I cut enough underlay to fill it.'

He showed me a battered page of A4 paper which had been repaired so many times with sellotape that it was laminated. On it, set out in biro like a times table, was scrawled all the possible customer room sizes between 2m × 3m, up to 8m × 8m, and he asked me to point to one.

'Well, it's not actually going in a room,' I confessed, 'but I've measured up and know that I need 3 square metres.'

There was a long pause.

'What happens,' he said, in a tone which let me know that this would be the last time he was going explain this to me, 'is that you tell me the size of your room, and I look it up on here...'

There was a long silence whilst we considered how we had arrived at this impasse – he was the one, very cleverly, to hit on it. He pointed his finger at me.

'*Your* trouble is you haven't got a room.'

'Could you give me enough for a room of 3 × 1?' I tried.

'3 × 1?'

'Yes... please.'

He looked at the paper – that room size wasn't on there.

He turned to his colleague who had spent the last five minutes trying to attach a yellow Post-it note reading *Mrs Thompson* to the back of a carpet, but it kept falling off.

'This man wants underlay for a room 3 × 1,' he said, 'but it's not on here.' At that his colleague look startled, having forgotten that he shared the planet with other people.

The second man unrolled some underlay, measured it at 2.5 metres, and sent the first off to see if he could find a pair of scissors. A minute later, from across the department, came a shout from my assistant, who was holding a pair of carpet scissors above his head.

'These them?'

'They got *Carpets* written on them?'

'Yeah.'

'Yeah.'

The second man kept his finger on a place on the underlay until the first had returned.

'Just here...'

'What – there?'

'Yeah – there.'

The second man started entering digits into a calculator – scrawled some numbers onto a yellow Post-it note, and stuck it to the back of my underlay.

'Take that to the till,' he ordered.

I turned to leave, caught the Post-it note as it came unglued, and left.

With the underlay stapled to the inside of the engine box, Linda and I were able to hold a conversation whilst the engine was running – which hailed in a new era.

The brilliant thing about being in Falmouth – one of the biggest natural harbours in the world – is that you can go sailing every day. We've taken non-sailing guests out in winds of Force 9 with a squiffy-little triple reefed main, and reefed staysail – a *slab-reefed* staysail, for heavens sake! – and enjoyed thrilling sails within the estuary. All made possible by the fact that the water remains relatively calm. We're heeled well over, of course, but the decks are dry, and the movement of the boat is exhilarating without being frightening. But even in a harbour accidents will happen and we nearly had our own disaster in October when Linda's sister and family came to visit, and we least expected it.

The wind wasn't blowing that hard. In fact, it was a perfect day for a family sail. There were seven of us on board – four adults and three children aged between 9 and 15. Late morning found us sweeping upriver – against the stream and with the wind behind us – toward a sandbank which chokes off three-quarters of the width of the river, leaving a passage of about 100m through which all craft are obliged to pass. Immediately after that the river swings to the right. That's where we'd have to gybe. Gybing is everybody's least favourite manoeuvre, having such capacity for things to go wrong as you heave the mainsail from one side of the boat – where it has been stretched out like a bird's wing – to the other. At some point during the manoeuvre the wind gets round the 'wrong' side of the cloth, slams everything over, and tries to pull the mast out of the boat.

We'd just got ourselves past the sandbank and had started to turn. Everybody had something to do – some were pulling on ropes, others letting theirs go – and to make room for all these new bodies Linda and I had moved from our usual positions to unfamiliar ones much further aft. We got through it all right, though I remember hearing a splash at the height of our activity. We'd just settled our boat onto the new course when it occurred to me that something was amiss. I was sure that there was a vacant space in my periphery vision which had a moment earlier been occupied by a body. Putting two and two together, I scanned the faces around me and came to the conclusion that one was missing.

'Where's Linda?' I asked.

The question was met with silence – no one knew, but the expression on the faces of the two younger boys told me that they wished permission to speak, and their eyes alternated between me and the water behind us. I turned to look over my shoulder and was just in time to see a pair of hands emerge through the foam, clutching a rope, rising in slow motion from the turbulent depths below. I instantly recognised the rope. Moments later a head appeared which I felt certain belonged to my wife. I leapt up to grab the other end of the rope she was holding, pulled at it hand-over-hand until she was alongside, and then called Steve's name. Steve is a 'bricky' and no stranger to lifting weights. Our first pull had Linda upside down in the cockpit – she was shocked, but otherwise none the worse for her experience, and already giving orders.

We waved goodbye to Sandra, Steve and the children the following day knowing we'd given them a weekend to remember. For our part, it had been an enjoyable social whirl of activity. They would be our last visitors of the year. Now we could relax, and there was a strange relief from knowing that all our summer work was done, and that we could look forward to a slow winter cosied up by the fire.

This winter would surely not be as wild as the last, and all we had to do was drop our anchor at the foot of a tree-covered hill for the protection it offered against a gale of wind, row ashore to choose the best, driest firewood, and stretch our legs along coastal paths, filling our lungs with bracing sea air.

13 FOUR COLLISIONS AND A REMOVAL

'HOW ARE YOU DOING, CURLY?' We hadn't seen him for two years. Curly lived in perfect contentment alone on a small boat with no heating – a freegan, and a minimalist.

'OK,' he said, but there were no smiles.

'What are you up to?'

'Haven't you heard?' he said.

'Heard what?'

The mood changed.

Unbeknown to us, Curly's boat had caught fire two nights previously, burning to the waterline, then sinking. He'd been lucky to get out alive. He wasn't sure exactly what had happened but he'd gone to bed leaving a candle burning – it was his only form of lighting – and woken to find himself trapped by flames. His only way out was to run through the fire and tumble overboard, choking, into a dinghy, unhitch his line and row far away from the heat. His boat, and the few things it contained, was everything he owned, so it struck a chord with us particularly. But even when you share an experience, what can you say to someone who has lost everything?

'What are you going to do now?'

'I don't know. I'm staying with friends ashore while I work all that out.'

Curly had arrived in Cornwall from the Midlands, bought himself a tiny boat, and taught himself to sail it. He'd seemed very happy living on the water, but now that he had no boat, we felt sure when we said our awkward goodbyes that we wouldn't be seeing him again.

A couple of weeks later I was chatting to someone about the places you can still find old wooden boats hidden up creeks in the South West, and it reminded me of another man – Ian – who I hadn't seen since arriving back. I would have noticed him if I'd passed him in the street because he had a very distinctive appearance: tall with a long gait, dreadlocks down to the backs of his knees, and nervous eyes.

Old wooden boats, if they still float and keep out the rain – and sometimes even if they don't – are home to 'alternative', unusual or eccentric people. Facts are facts. No conventional family of four ever moved from a Barratt Home into a Brixham trawler built in 1910. Living on old boats we've met half-mad Ancient Mariners, wiry graduates from boatbuilding colleges, bespectacled graduates from Cambridge University, and plenty of sea gypsies – some of whom were wild and unwashed, and some of whom were softly spoken, deferential, and only returned occasionally to the area from one of their serial seven-year circumnavigations. One of them was a chap called Graham, and that was all we knew about him. We'd chat to him for half an hour and wind up with:

'Where are you heading next?'

'Haven't really made my mind up – probably Vanua Levu.'

'Oh, OK...' we'd say, pretending we knew where that was. Then we wouldn't see him for years.

Ian's appearance was certainly 'wild'. He wasn't unwashed, but there's only so much you can do when your skin is like boot-leather. You'd see him striding through town on his way to work at the docks, or decanting other people's beer into his own glass in the pub at night when they weren't looking.

'Where's Ian? Haven't seen him for a while.'

'Ian who?'

'I don't know his surname. That tall dark-haired chap with the Rastafarian hairdo. Lives on a boat in Penryn and works at the docks.'

'He drowned!'

'Drowned? How did that happen?'

'No one knows. They found him one morning floating face down in the water alongside his boat with a large dent in his head.'

'What, was he drunk or something?'

'Someone might have hit him over the head with a big stick... some people say.'

'What do the police say?'

'Well, they're not bothered, are they?'

There are eccentric, sometimes challenging people in every harbour, who are different from us, and, if we're being honest, we think we can do without them. But when they're gone, we miss them. *Never send to know for whom the bell tolls; it tolls for thee.* – John Donne (1572–1631)

Falmouth Harbour had been cleared for a shipping movement. Four tugs were manoeuvring a luxury passenger liner up to the dock using only pieces of string, and around the perimeter of the operation, harbour authority craft marshalled the area, racing toward any pleasure boats daft enough to stray into the danger zone, then escorting them out of the way with a few choice words. It's amazing to see the size of the vessels they can swing past the town quay and into the docks. Some of them, as they go past, I'll swear make the town go dark.

We were at a mooring in the harbour, hidden deep within hundreds of other moorings, whilst all this was going on. The breeze blew from the town – which we faced – and the port operation was taking place about a hundred yards behind us. When I thought the action was coming to a close I hoisted sail. Dave, on his yacht *Thursday's Child* nearby, settled into his cockpit seat to watch us leave, knowing that he would either witness a manoeuvre well done, or a disaster. There's no middle way with us. We dropped the mooring, sailed ahead into a clearing left by a couple of empty moorings, and then performed a rather neat 180 degree turn-on-the-spot, all powered by the wind. So far, so good. That 'stationary' turn, and the downwind leg which followed it, required the main boom to be let off as far as it would go, reaching out far over the side of our boat, an arrangement which proved to be our downfall. The sail filled powerfully, driving us on through moored vessels and out toward open water, where the shipping movement was all but over and only the harbour launches remained idly floating at their stations, awaiting the instruction to 'stand down'.

180 degree turn

Our course took us between two moored vessels which were closer together than I thought. I reckoned that we would pass between them with just a foot or two to spare. What I hadn't factored in was that because our boom was bowsed far out-board, we were considerably wider than normal. Spotting my mistake just ahead of the collision, I spent the few moments remaining to me hauling the boom back in, all too late unfortunately, and our boom banged into the steel-wire stay supporting the mast of the vessel on our left. The steel wire zipped along our boom's varnish-work until it met a fitting. There it snagged. By this time we were sailing quite fast and everything was happening quickly. Giving the tangled vessel a good yank, I remember seeing its mast – like a sword – cross ours. A very honourable way to begin a duel. We wrenched at the other boat, which in turn tugged its mooring rope taut until the moment something had to give. I heard an almighty twang but was so busy just then that I couldn't turn to see what disaster I had left astern. When I did have time to look over my shoulder, expecting to see their mast following us through the water, all seemed taut and upright as the yacht rushed back to its spot, pulled by its own mooring buoy.

Naturally enough I hoped my collision might go unnoticed. Quite the opposite: we didn't have our radio on, but Dave told me later that the VHF boomed into life with an instruction to one of the harbour authority craft to go and check the vessel whose rigging we'd just twanged for damage. A minute or two later the radio crackled back into life with the welcome news that no damage had been caused, so they never sent the pursuit vessel, and we sailed on to our freedom. I was lucky to get away with that. The experience, you would think, should have clipped my wings – made me think twice about handling our boat under sail at close quarters – but you don't learn a new skill by never making mistakes.

We sailed into the Helford River to the spot known as Frenchman's Creek – made famous by Daphne du Maurier – and plonked our anchor down in pride of place. There are sightseeing trips to this spot from Falmouth. We remembered that fact as we were settling down to bake some Cornish pasties I'd made, to see how close I could get to the real thing. We became aware of a low growling noise outside, and noticed, deep in the belly of our boat, that things had grown a little bit darker in spite of the fact that the paraffin cooker was playing up again, and was belching great balls of yellow flame into the air. We can't see anything that's in front of us or behind us when we're down below in our accommodation because we haven't got any windows in those two directions. We'd checked the portholes at the sides to see what was going on, and there was nothing abeam, so we climbed the companion steps to find one of the Falmouth tripper boats towering over us, stationary, ten feet from our stern. All its passengers, imagining that we were part of the tour, had arranged themselves along the railings and looked down on us to see if they could see our pasties.

The skipper was high up on his bridge. He opened the door and walked out. 'So this is where you're hiding. Haven't seen you for ages. Where you been?'

'Scotland! We were going to come back last year but got stuck in the pack-ice.'

'Should think you did. What you wanna go Scotland for?'

'It's lovely...'

'I know – been there myself.'

'Where?'

'Oh, some bloody place – Loch something I think twas...'

'That narrows it down... Ness?'

'No-o-o... I've 'eard of that one, mind.'

'Lomond?'

'Lomond... yeah, might be. Anyhow – now ya back, don't go away again without asking.'

With that, and a great rumble from his engine, he powered away to continue his tour.

Those Cornish pasties were great. I don't get enough pastry in my diet.

The following morning was sunny and a playful breeze blew from the east, in our faces as we looked downriver and straight out to sea. We hauled up the huge mainsail. I wouldn't be able to get that mainsail up if I was any thinner, or lighter.

It weighs nearly as much as I do. To raise it I leap into the air and grab two ropes as high up as I can when I'm at my zenith – they're attached to each end of the gaff – then I fold my legs up behind me and use my body as a counterweight, like the sash cord in an old window. As I sink slowly to the deck, I watch the gaff reluctantly rise. By the time it's at full hoist, I'm ready for my bait – as they say in Scotland, to mean elevenses. Next, the jib unfurled with a shudder, and I pushed the tiller over to move the bow off to one side, and fill the sail with wind. The incoming tide was against us, stretching out our anchor chain. The bow fell off to port. We began to move ahead until a few seconds later when our anchor chain was straining taut, off to starboard, dripping at the surface of the water. We stalled for a moment, the weight of chain tacked the boat, we threw the tiller over to agree with it, and sailed up to the anchor, gathering slack chain hand-over-hand as we went. Just before the chain was straight up and down, and we were directly over the anchor, I threw a couple of turns of chain around the Samson post, we sailed over the anchor's head, and our momentum pulled it out of the ground as though it were a spade in the sand.

Ahead of us in the river across which we began to tack, we could see the transoms of a couple of hundred yachts, all swaying to their moorings. They seemed impenetrable, but we would have to stitch a zigzag course through them to get beyond the moorings, and out to sea. All we could do for now was enter the pack, diagonally, for our first stitch, and see where that took us. Spotting an empty mooring off to the left, we decided to head for it and use the space it offered to make our first turn. Success. We settled onto our new diagonal course, throwing glances ahead to see if a route through the pack suggested itself. Our view was a wall of white hulls with, here and there, some teeny gaps between them – in some places the gaps were more generous – so we headed for those, and climbed through them one by one until we reached the other side.

When we see a gap, we've learnt to aim directly amidships of the boat we intend to pass behind – as though we mean to sink it – and then only at the last minute steer round its stern... that way if the wind suddenly fails, we've bought ourselves a bit of time by being upwind, and upstream, of our chosen gap.

As the adventure wore on, with each new problem resolving itself at the last moment, with both of us on lookout, and Linda repeating the words 'Oh God... Oh God' every time she spotted something she didn't like, we picked our way through the entire fleet, dealing only with the situation immediately at hand, and leaving the future to take care of itself. Our penultimate tack took us intimately close to a boat whose crew were chatting over breakfast in their cockpit; so close in fact that they could have buttered us each a croissant, offered us a choice of preserves, and handed it over. Coming so close, it felt as though we were intruding on their privacy, and their chatter ebbed away to silence. It's hard to invent a new and diverting topic of conversation when your attention has been drawn to the sharp end of a bowsprit which is pointing straight for you, and to a growing wall of canvas which is slowly robbing you of your view. No one spoke. Our own rapt attention was concentrated on avoiding their stern. Then a voice spoke at a volume which suggested we were all gathered around the same table:

'Beautiful! Absolutely lovely!'

'Thanks,' we squeaked, hoping our voices didn't give us away. These adrenalin-fuelled little voyages, inches from trouble, provide the excitement we miss when we're not cruising to new waters. We love handling our boat like it, but our hearts are in our mouths.

Quiet nights at anchor were interspersed with raucous ones at the Quayside Inn, where the sound of singing and laughter drifted far over the water. I don't know if bands have to audition to play there but the one in that night were so good I wondered why they hadn't 'made it'. That became a little clearer mid-evening when they'd played all their good ones and internecine disputes began breaking out about what to play next. The keyboard player ended the argument by playing his choice, only to be challenged by lead guitar playing something completely different, and at greater volume. Then the drummer

Arriving under sail

broke into a solo which neither of them could interrupt and which, if anything, was more exuberant than Animal's (off *The Muppets*). After several minutes of crashing cymbals, he leaped into the air, only to bang his head on one of the historic pub's low beams, and slumped back onto his stool, nursing his injury. Neither did the band seem certain about how to deal with the wiry and bearded old man of seventy who'd been allowed out on licence and was celebrating the fact by line-dancing up and down in front of the stage, listening to music he'd got on his MP3 player.

I missed Ian for not being there, helping himself to my beer when I wasn't looking, and saving me from a worse headache than the one I had coming.

Walking back to our boat in the wee hours, along the visitor's pontoon, I'd got just enough sense to wonder why there were wet footprints on the teak boards, and followed them under the sulphur light. Some late-night reveller who lives on the other side of the estuary had obviously missed the last bus home, and tried to nick some unfortunate chap's dinghy, but had got their comeuppance – they must have nicked a real crap-heap of a dinghy and been tipped in by it. With that, in my periphery vision I noticed our dinghy, upside down in the water a few metres away. For a moment I felt quite insulted that they'd abandoned it as inadequate for their purpose, though they'd kept the beautifully crafted leathered oars I'd spent four days whittling to shape from choice poles of ash.

When I came to replace those oars I bought a cheap proprietary brand of oar made from white pine. No one has ever nicked those – you can't even *give* them away.

If we've got a favourite month on the river, it's September. The rush of the school summer holiday weeks are over, the air is one or two degrees cooler – and fresher for it – and the mornings hang shrouded with mist. At half past six one morning, as we lay to our anchor, miles upriver, we couldn't see the water in which we were floating; we seemed instead to be supported by a cloud of vapour. During breakfast the mist thinned, offering glimpses of the world around us, the branches which overhung the shore, then the fields beyond, and behind us, four boats at anchor formed a line. As the tide crept past us like molten silver, I walked up to the anchor, impatient to get away. The engine wasn't working, there was no wind, and the only thing going our way was the tide. Looking at our hanging chain, I was interested to notice a fly on the water, and followed him all the way back to the stern to get a feel for how fast the water was ebbing, and how long it might take the fly – and us if we lifted our anchor – to arrive in Falmouth.

I'd dismantled part of the engine, and a replacement part was waiting for me in the harbour office, if only I could get there. Although there wasn't a breath of wind this far upriver, amongst the trees, we might find a puff further down if we weighed anchor and drifted along with the fly. The only impediment to the scheme was the four boats at anchor behind us, and the danger of drifting into them. Fortunately we'd anchored in this spot so many times that we knew there was a slight flaw in the ebbing stream at this point in the river. Instead of flowing parallel with the banks it swung out toward the beach on our port hand, before sweeping back again into the deep water channel. If I pulled the anchor chain in quickly, and cast the bow off to port, we might ride the tide and go wide of all four boats, whose owners would still be tucked in their beds at such an early hour on a Monday morning.

The anchor and chain clanged home. I walked back to the tiller and, looking ahead, noticed that *Caol Ila* had decided to point her nose to starboard against my wishes. It would have been nothing to correct it, yet on the spur of the moment I decided to stick with the new plan. Of course, the tidal stream, which might have carried us clear to port, carried us instead directly into the boat behind, who happened to be our friends John and Pam. They arrived on deck in their pyjamas.

'Sorry about this, John.'

'Don't worry, Justin,' he said.

Pam smiled, but I could see that this was a black mark against me.

John and Pam fended us off, walking us to the back of their boat, and then gave us a helpful shove out to starboard. There the tide got hold of us once more, and moments later delivered us alongside the boat behind them.

'Sorry about this,' I said, when the owners came on deck, having been woken by the commotion. 'We haven't got an engine.'

They smiled, and walked us to the stern of their boat. They too gave us a helpful shove to starboard.

'Morning, Mark,' I said when we hit Mark and Anne's boat. 'Sorry about this.'

'Don't worry, mate. Not a problem. Where are you off to?'

'Falmouth. Should be there by Wednesday...'

Mark and Anne walked us to the back of their boat, all smiles as usual, and they too gave us a helpful shove.

The people on the fourth boat were already at their bow, smiling thin smiles.

'Sorry to keep you waiting...' I said, as we hit their boat.

'Do you want to tie alongside 'til you get yourselves sorted out?'

'That's kind of you but we've got to press on or we'll miss the tide.'

Privately my anxiety was rising because the next flaw in the stream swept over to a pontoon on which there were a *dozen* boats. By some miracle a wind – so light it wouldn't have extinguished the flame of a candle – wafted into our sails and allowed us to clear the pontoon.

Four hundred yards further on we found ourselves being swept toward the 12,000-ton vessel *Tamamima* on her lay-up mooring – in so many ways an unmissable feature of the narrow river hereabouts. Just then the harbour master's launch came around the corner, manned by two young chaps – students dressed for a hot day on the water in their shorts and sunglasses, skin glistening with oil. We flagged them down and asked if they could give us a tow downriver, to which they cheerfully agreed, and in any case seemed very much like the sort of lads who enjoyed starting their day with a tug-job. They caught our rope, made it fast, wound up their engines, and then reclined coolly in their seats as they paraded us downriver to where a breeze stirred on the face of the water.

On the first of October, the river falls silent. It's the first day of winter as far as mooring fees are concerned, and everyone without a permanent berth rushes into marinas to take up winter residence until the following April. For us, it feels as though we can have the river to ourselves for the next six months, sharing it only with a few commercial craft going about their business: the environment agency testing water quality, harbour authority craft, survey vessels, and the oyster dredgers who can only fish under their rags of sail between October and March.

Four oyster dredgers

We had to fly up to Scotland for a couple of weeks later in the month because Linda's mum wasn't very well, and left our boat on our favourite upriver pontoon. We hadn't been away long when we got a call from someone to say our mast had broken. Our caller had been staying on his boat, moored just behind us, the previous night when the wind had blown 'Nines and Tens'. A part of our jib had got unfurled and was flogging (will we ever learn?) so he'd gone on board at one o'clock on a dark night to try to get it down. What he couldn't have known was that unless he released a wire stay that goes to the topmast, first, he'd break the mast... and did.

We arrived back home to find – not for the first time – lengths of broken timber with rope lashed neatly around them, all tidily stowed on deck, as though that's how our spars were usually stored.

We were just scratching our heads, staring at the bits, when someone came up to us.

'I reckon you 'ad a lucky escape!' he said.

'Perhaps, but it will take days – even weeks – to fix all this!'

'Eh?' he said, noticing the splintered wood for the first time. 'No – I didn't mean that...' And went on to tell us how he'd been night fishing a few days back, in an open boat tied to this very pontoon. He was just lying back looking at the stars when he heard a boat arrive, after midnight, at the pontoon, saw a couple of guys get out, looking a bit suspicious, wandering up and down next to our boat, and then watched as they climbed on board.

With that the fisherman got out of his boat and crept silently along the pontoon, finally arriving alongside, then shouting: 'Woss on, then, boys?!'

'You should have seen them jump! "Oh nothin'," they says, then their legs turned to jelly. They almost fell in the water to get away! And off they howled!'

Repairing a 50ft (15m) mast, in the 'bush', with limited tools, was a problem that baffled me all that day and most of the next.

Then a mussel fisherman motored past in his yellow dungarees. 'If you need a hand getting your mast down, my crane'll probably do it.'

A mile downriver was a mussel farm – clumpy-looking timber rafts, with PVC drums for floats, supported rows and rows of what looked like onion nets, but were filled with juvenile mussel 'spats'. Pretty soon they grow until the raft is barely able to support their weight, the whole apparatus almost submerged to the strain of tens of tons of mussels, each bag of which can only be lifted by a floating crane.

A few weeks before our mast incident I'd seen the mussel man drifting miserably past in his boat. I was moored in the same spot as we now occupied with our broken mast.

'Can you chuck me a line?' he yelled from so far across the river that I could only just make out what he was saying, and followed it with a despairing laugh – because at that distance you'd need a helluva long line, and a super-human chuck.

'What's the problem?'

'Bastard outboard won't work.'

'I'll come and get you.'

I untied the mooring lines, motored out to get him, and then towed him back downriver from whence he came, and cast him off at the slipway where he kept his car. He wanted to return the favour, hence the mast-craning offer. His crane wasn't tall, but if he grabbed the 38ft stump that we had left, somewhere about the halfway mark, we thought we might be able to manhandle it to the deck. That plan was executed without a hitch.

The next piece of the jigsaw fell into place when I remembered having stored a couple of baulks of stout timber in an abandoned building on the shore. I'd stumbled across the building by accident, years earlier, whilst walking off-piste. It was hidden by the twisted stems and dense foliage of a mature ivy, which had left only a part of the blue-painted door visible. I couldn't find the building at first when I went in search of it but when I pushed at the door, un-snagging the little ivy suckers, I found that inside it was still dry; there were crisp brown leaves on the cement floor, and my timber was waiting for me. I couldn't even remember who'd given me the timber, but it was 'A' grade.

Repairing a 50ft mast which had snapped 12ft along its length is easier than you think: if you broke a pencil one quarter along its length the repair would be identical – you'd take a penknife and, working only from two sides, shave both the broken ends until all the damaged wood was removed and you were left with a chisel-edge on each. Laying the two ends of your pencil on a table with their edges together, all that's needed to glue them together would be a piece of wood shaped not unlike one of those old-fashioned wooden clothes-pegs. Those two pieces of timber I'd laid up in the building ashore were going to be my (giant) clothes pegs.

There was a hitch, of course. Although our mast is 50ft long, the pontoons on which I was going to work were only 40. The mast would have to straddle two pontoons, and the trouble with that plan was, every time the tide turned, the pontoons curved with the new tide like the roofs of a train going round a bend, whereas the mast needed to be kept dead straight for two days until the glue had set. The answer to the problem came to me suddenly, and in the middle of the night, so that I sat bolt upright in bed.

With both damaged ends of my mast shaved into scarfs, and the mating surfaces of my laid-up timber planed to match them (so accurately that I can't take credit for the work – the spirit of an old sea carpenter who had drowned hereabouts was standing over me, guiding my hand) I supported 40ft of the mast on blocks, from one single pontoon. The last 12ft were airborne above the second pontoon: in order to support that, I ran a rope the length of the mast, tied it top and bottom, and then, by erecting a forked stick – like the stick that supports a sagging clothes-line, and which crane-operators would know as a jib strut – then draping the rope over the stick, I found I could adjust the angle of the glued end with millimetre accuracy by adjusting the tension in the rope. Not only that but I found that the arrangement as a whole tended to pull my glued joint together.

The job took just over a week, the weather remained fair, the pontoon was covered in planer-shavings for the second time in three years, and passing shipping (there was a coaster collecting scrap metal for Germany, and a calcified-seaweed dredger came up most days) would monitor progress through their binoculars, then give me a long blast of approval with their horn, even stepping outside the bridge to wave their approval when they could see I was on the right track. When the job was complete, the skipper of the scrap-metal boat – which was unfeasibly long for the twists and turns of the river he navigated – took time out from the intricacies of the task he had on hand to step out onto the flying bridge, remove his hat, and bow to his knees as he passed.

With the glue dry, I took hold of the masthead, bounced it until the whole mast flexed, and knew the joints were beyond doubt. I lifted the mast on board – though not without difficulty, since Linda was away for a few days – and then motored down to Mylor Harbour, where they have a hand-operated mast-crane capable of handling masts a lot longer than ours. For a small consideration they hoisted my new mast upright and left me to set up the rig. *Caol Ila* was a sailing vessel once more.

Binoculars have a hard life on board a boat – or at least they do on our boat. I designed and built a kind of a binocular-holder which was screwed it to the underside of the roof so that anyone in the cockpit could just feel through the hatch and grab them at a moment's notice. The trouble is that there's a knack to putting them back – the neck-strap has to be folded around them in a certain way, and neither of us can remember which way it is. But I'm more patient than Linda. I don't mind standing there for ten minutes to find out by trial and error how it all goes back. Linda's one of those people who always needs to be getting on with the next thing, whereas I'm OK spending my life doing nothing. Anyway, this isn't about *blame* so there's no point in mentioning names, but Linda had put the binoculars back the wrong way, and the next time we sailed over on our ear and bounced on a wave, the binoculars fell against the engine box, split down the middle, and solved the problem of *sharing* a pair of binoculars by giving us a monocular each.

I went back to the department store where I bought my under-felt – they sell binoculars too – and peered into the locked glass cabinet in which are stored goods of more than £20 in value. There were three pairs displayed for sale. I asked to see the £28 pair. The assistant looked me up and down to assess whether I was the sort of person who *had* £28, gave me the benefit of the doubt, and then unlocked the cabinet, allowing its door to swing open on her side of the counter. Then she froze, staring irritably at its shelves. After a while I realised that this was her way of communicating to a customer that she now required more information. I pointed to the pair in which I was interested: tiny 'compact' binoculars, where the object lens is identical, or nearly identical in size to the image lens.

'Can I have a look at those?' I said, pointing.

'May...'

'Sorry?'

'*May* I have a look...'

She placed them on the counter where I could reach them. I turned them over in my hands, baffled by which end you were supposed to put to your eyes, so I took pot luck. At first I couldn't see anything at all because they were folded so neatly they didn't stretch across my nose. I opened them out, put them to my eyes, and suddenly everything seemed much further away. I amused myself by scanning the walls to see how much bigger the shop became. Then I noticed a hand rushing toward my face from about half-a-mile away. In no time it reached me and snatched the binoculars from my eyes, turned them end for end, and then shoved them back into my face. It was the assistant, performing a random act of kindness. She curled her lip at the ceiling, rolled her eyes, then slumped on the counter, appearing to demand of fate why she had been born onto a planet of idiots. I wasn't fond of the 'compact' binoculars and wanted to see a standard pair on the next shelf, but daren't ask because when I handed back the compacts she placed them back into the cabinet, locked it and then stared through me.

For our grocery shopping, we walked along quiet country roads whose hedges shook with each new blast of wind. As we passed, birds sheltering within threw themselves into the swirling air to be torn away across the fields and dive for cover into the hedge on the other side. These stragglers would soon be migrating to avoid the rude winter. I wished I could go with them.

As the weeks rolled by, the sight of a boat on the river became a rare thing. For little adventures we'd take our boat to Truro on spring tides. It's a meandering journey which follows narrow channels, unseen beneath the muddy water. On the outskirts of the town the channel took us right to the railings of a path where a group of drunks shouted at us. Some had dogs who barked at us, but the commotion was so loud, with everyone shouting at once, we didn't know if this was a greeting or a defence. We moored alongside the town quay, waved up to the staff of a plush new office who'd crowded to the window having noticed our mast go past, and then we tied our mast in to a huge steel bollard so that the boat wouldn't fall away from the quay when the tide went out.

Linda had work as a 'bank' health visitor, filling in a couple of days a week for someone on long-term sick leave. It was convenient sometimes to be moored here as there was a shower on the quay – one of those portable showers that look like a *Doctor Who* police box in blue plastic, though when we stepped inside, it was actually *smaller* on the inside.

I settled down to do some illustration work, which was much easier now we could plug into the mains electricity and have all the lights on at once without worrying about our batteries. A couple of other boats were live-aboards, though they left early and came home late. The atmosphere of the place, particularly when the tide went out – leaving muddy ooze studded with shopping trolleys, parking cones, cans and bottles – was a bit depressing. Well, more than a bit.

I met one of our neighbours one day, a woman in her early thirties. We chatted for a while, comparing live-aboard notes.

'How do you mean... *downriver*?' she asked me when I told her where we spent most of our winter. 'There's nothing there...'

I was struck by her appearance. Her face, to my mind, had a timeless quality, putting me in mind of a photograph taken in the 1800s, which you might see in a folk museum. Her style and freshness – rosy cheeked, shortish curly hair of mousy-brown, square-shouldered and at the height of her womanly powers – was ideal for a drawing I was working on featuring a fisherwife. I mentioned that I was an illustrator, and that if ever she had the time I wished she would model for me. She gave me a look as much as to say 'Do you imagine I was born yesterday?' and the conversation didn't survive long after that.

Fisherwife

The next day whilst Linda was at work I had a surprise visit from a chap who we'd met together with his girlfriend on a pub-lunch outing a couple of weeks earlier. We were introduced by mutual friends because he and his girlfriend were emigrating to Scotland and we, of course, were experts on Scotland.

He arrived now with his toddler daughter, his charge for the day, lifted her out of her buggy and passed her down to me. Her nose and face were glistening with snot from a streaming cold. Below decks I made some tea whilst she romped about on the soft furnishings. I have to confess that from where I stand the world seems to fall neatly into two sorts of people – those for whom children can do no wrong, and me. What with her outdoor shoes trotting about on our sofa, and snotty face against the seat-backs, I could scarcely concentrate on the conversation out of a prissy concern for our cushions.

'She absolutely loves books!' her dad told me, beaming with pride, whilst his daughter clawed at our bookshelf, trying to pull one free.

'Are you looking forward to moving to Scotland?'

'Can't wait. Sold everything. Loaded the van. Leaving on Tuesday.'

'No regrets about leaving the surf of Newquay behind?'

'Up there it's better – better everything. Bought a shop. Got a house. Can't wait.'

'What about your wife, or..?'

'She can't wait either.'

He was so enthusiastic about the move, so full of praise for Scotland as a country of opportunity, that I began to wonder if we should ever have come back down south. I didn't have any trouble imagining that the surf is very good up there – or at least, that the waves are big – but apparently surfers make nothing of finning out into the Minch, summer and winter, to take advantage of it. I struggled to picture that bit.

His daughter pulled a cloth-bound book from the shelf.

'See! I told you! I don't know where she gets it from but she absolutely loves books! Can she have a look at that one?'

'Er... yes.'

She opened it in the middle, wrapped it around her face, and wiped her nose and cheeks on its crisp old parchment. Her dad stood aghast, watching for his opportunity, and when it came, took the book from her to look at the front cover:

'*The Letters of Charles Lamb: Vol 1*,' he read aloud, and handed it back to her, shaking his head. 'Where *does* she get it from?'

I took a number of my drawings into a gallery in Truro and asked the owner if he would mind taking a look at them. He didn't appear to be the kind of man to suffer fools gladly, and even though he seemed ten years younger than me, reminded me of one of my schoolmasters in his Harris tweed jacket and Bakelite glasses, made in an era when plastic was still an experimental material.

'Not at all,' he said, without the least hesitation, and cleared a space on the counter for me to lay down my portfolio, which he opened, tucked one arm behind his back and began leafing through in silence, eyebrows at full hoist.

'Right,' he said when he had viewed the last one without ever coming close to being impressed. 'These are not commercial.'

'How do you mean?'

'You will *never* sell any.'

'Oh... OK... would you be prepared to try one or two of them?'

'It would be useless, absolutely useless... I'll give it to you – you *can* draw, but you're wasting your time on these.'

It was impossible not to admire his decisiveness. As he handed back my portfolio he wore the warm smile of a man who had saved a fellow artist from a lifetime of pointless struggle.

We had a spell ashore after that, in a house, but it wasn't a success. I arranged to help a chap complete a house he was building in return for the use of a cottage which had been leased to him, or which he said had been leased to him. I found myself working most days, and then he handed me bills, which I understood were included in our arrangement, so I had to get more work to pay those. Thankfully the arrangement came to a close when the lessee's agent knocked on our door one dark evening and told us we would have to leave because our acquaintance had no right to sub-let the house.

He was a great churchgoer, I recall, giving him an advantage over people who never went to church, and who consequently never thought to look for the Devil in the detail. Moving back on board after six weeks ashore, life seemed very uncomplicated once more.

14 PRESIDENT VISITS FISH MARKET

WE WERE PLANNING TO SPEND THE SUMMER IN FRANCE, but still had to find work to replenish the treasury. Just in time a roofing job came up on a medieval house in Hereford, accommodation thrown in. And since the house was owned as a retreat by our hippie friends Tim and Lindy – the ones who'd stayed with us on their honeymoon in Scotland – and they would be living in the house during the roof-works, we were to have more lovage salads than most folk have a hope of enjoying in a lifetime.

The Weald and Downland Open Air Museum in Sussex is my favourite day out – they've got loads of medieval houses there, but they *charge* you to go in, and then lock you out of their grounds at 5. With this job we'd get *paid* to stay in a medieval house for three weeks! We lashed our boat to a pontoon, doubled-up the lines, then rowed ashore, hiding our dinghy amongst the trees.

Our banger sewed its way over the hills between Cornwall and Herefordshire until we found a field gate which fitted the description, swung it open, and bounced along a track until it began to plunge down into a bottomless valley. We parked under the shade of a tree, jammed a stone in front of the wheels because the handbrake wasn't too clever, and then continued on foot, carrying our bags down a rutted woodland track until we came upon a half-timbered medieval house which seemed startled that we'd discovered the secret of its location. Being the first to arrive we let ourselves in with a key, the hiding place of which had been described to us with the euphemism 'in case we're late...'

A description of the house better start with what it *had:* it had one cold-water tap, and the windows were glazed – those were its concessions to modernity. It *didn't* have electricity, a phone, a loo, central heating, neighbours, or a road. And it had no postal service – because it didn't have an address.

Tim and Lindy arrived full of apologies, shaking their heads in disbelief, absolutely at a loss to explain how it was that they were four hours late. Another half-hour was consumed on the doorstep, reconstructing the events which led up to their late arrival, from which they produced the conclusion that there were several possible causes: firstly, they were still at home ten minutes after we'd arranged to meet; secondly, they hadn't allowed for the fact that it would take *time* to drive the two hundred miles between there and here; and finally, they'd stopped to do some shopping in two towns on the way.

'Speaking of which – look! We found the most amazing carrot cake!'

We sprawled in the garden on a hot afternoon, drinking cups of organic tea with bits floating in it, and eating slices of really good carrot cake, until I wondered out loud if I might climb onto the roof for a reconnoitre.

'Great idea – I'll get changed and join you,' Tim called.

Ten minutes later, as I squatted on the roof, I heard his boots on the ladder as he climbed aloft, making good-to-be-alive noises as he came.

'How are you getting on?' he asked when he reached me, kneeling in the valley.

'Badly' would have been the honest answer, but I've noticed that people don't like to hear that sort of thing when you've come to do their roof – they prefer you to be optimistic and hopeful, and to give voice to that optimism in a sing-songy kind of way. I was intimidated by the huge slabs of stone with which the house had been roofed and which you usually only see buried in the undergrowth in a lost graveyard. Amazingly these stones were held in place by tiny oak pegs, hooked over flimsy battens. Recognising that Tim's arrival was a pivotal moment in the job, I'd been rehearsing something positive to say, and turned to say it when to my surprise I found myself face to face with his penis, nestled in what appeared to be a tangle of 13amp fuse wire.

I jumped back in horror and only then noticed he was naked except for a pair of work boots.

When our eyes met he raised his eyebrows twice, as if to say, 'What do you think of that, then?' I stumbled back to give myself a bit more room, composed myself, then turned to face him once more with a nonchalant expression, as much as to say that this was the kind of environment I was used to working in, and only gave myself away when I lost balance and nearly slid off the roof.

An awkward hour later, during which we'd been passing each other slates and working out a numbering system, I heard a tuneful voice drift up from below with the information that 'Coffee was ready'.

I couldn't get down that ladder fast enough and rushed indoors to wash my hands, but having been working in brilliant sunshine on the roof, I found the house pitch-dark and couldn't see anything, and so navigated by memory, feeling my way to where I remembered the sink was situated. As I groped through the darkness I touched something soft which jumped and squealed with surprise. I recognised the squeal, and the movement allowed my eyes to discern Lindy, in silhouette, washing dishes, with her breasts swinging heavily over the sink.

What we hadn't remembered about Tim and Lindy was that they were naturists. In fact I don't think we'd realised it until then. And it wasn't like they were dabbling with it as an experiment. You could tell by some of the poses they struck – brought about by everyday activities, like bending to pick up a spoon which had fallen to the floor – that they were very confident with it.

That evening friends of theirs came by for dinner, an attractive couple of about fifty to whom we introduced ourselves at the door. We shook hands.

'Isn't this weather glorious?'

'Absolutely gorgeous!'

'Too hot, really...'

'Yes! Too hot!'

Introductions over, they stripped off and threw their clothes to land scattered around the doormat.

'Ah – that's better!' they said with one voice when they were stark naked, and then smiled at us, as though that would be a trigger for something.

Linda and I ate with our clothes on, brows deeply knitted in concentration on the food on our plates. We've done a lot of things which mark us out as offbeat, but wearing clothes hadn't until then been one of them. Through the corner of my eye I kept looking out of the curtain-less window into the darkness beyond to see if I could see a figure lurking in the shadows – a peeping-tom, come to see what people look like with clothes on.

After dinner we were a bit more relaxed, so the naked man felt able to sit close to Linda on the couch in front of a roaring fire in the inglenook, pick up his guitar, and serenade her with a ballad. He shuffled in close. I hadn't seen my wife sitting next to a naked man before, so we were breaking new ground all over. Moving his whole body in a jolly sort of a way in time with the music, he set Linda swaying every time their torsos gently collided in time with the music, and in his lap his willy joined in the fun, throwing itself from side to side, landing with a little smack, first on one thigh, then the other...

The days were blistering-hot and there weren't two ways about it: working only in a pair of boots, Tim was getting a better tan than I was. Though I watched in horror one day, from indoors, when he'd just loaded the cement mixer, which was precariously balanced on a sheet of plywood using piles of bricks to level it. He went to pull the starter cord, putting the whole of his inconsiderable weight behind it. The machine rumbled into life, but wobbled eccentrically on its first rotation, collapsing one of the piles of bricks. The mixer knocked him backwards to the ground, then rolled nose-first on top of him with the barrel still turning. It was a frightening moment for Tim when he saw what was about to happen. And trapped on the ground with his legs wrapped round the revolving barrel you could see by the fact that his eyes were as wide as saucers that he was only too aware that his penis might become entangled in the fan belt... and certainly *would* have had it been of normal length.

We could have happily stayed with them under the spell of their medieval house for a year and it was with regret that we began to tidy up the site when the work was over. We all helped load the waste materials onto a trailer.

'Would you excuse me for a moment?' Lindy said, before walking around to the other side of the house. Moments later we heard a blood-curdling scream. We were about to leap to the rescue when we looked at Tim, who only rolled his eyes. Then Lindy reappeared, gave a single petitioning laugh, and threw a smile, first at Linda and then at me, then carried on with the work in hand. Sometimes we didn't like to ask...

Back in Cornwall, we arrived to find our dinghy leaning against the tree, covered with a reassuring scattering of woody debris, and its 'painter' – as sailors call the length of string by which you attach it to things – still coiled neatly on the upturned hull. It was windy. Overhead, the swaying branches sang – sometimes shrieked – in violent gusts of wind. The sun sparkled on the heaving backs of standing waves in the river, which collapsed suddenly into awful hollows, filled with white foam. We were used to seeing the river placidly flowing between its banks – today it looked like an ideal spot for white-water rafting, for anyone interested in that sort of thing. It was sobering to think that we would shortly be rowing across it. I packed everything around me in the dinghy, Linda got in, and we pushed off with our misgivings, and dry throats. In spite of how heavily we were laden, the wind caught the dinghy, scuttering it downwind whenever we reached the crest of a wave. In the troughs I worked hard to recover lost ground. Once we were exposed to the full power of the wind and waves it seemed an audacity to be out here rowing on it.

In one part of the river – perhaps over some spoil ground, or where the bottom shoals rapidly – the waves were highest.

A group of three of them will live in our memory for a very long time. We saw the trouble coming and turned the boat to face the wind and waves directly. I swung the oars forward in preparation for a really long stroke, as the first of them rolled up. I yelled for Linda to throw her weight forward, between my legs, and as we climbed the face of it, pulled on the oars. I remember how strange it was to see Linda far below me, her quick eyes reading my face as our boat came vertical. If we'd fallen sideways across the wave, we'd be lost. At the crest, without having taken a drop of water on board, we threw our weight backwards, to relieve the bow when it hit the trough which followed. There was a second similar wave, then a third which I didn't expect to get over. The third in the series always seems to be the biggest, perhaps because it's preceded by the deepest trough. As we climbed it, it broke, sending boiling foam all around us, singing as the bubbles burst whilst we bounced around in its chaos. The wave rolled onwards, the white foam evaporated to reveal solid water, and we turned the boat for home.

At the pontoon we recognised a lot of the faces that swarmed us silently, arms reaching out to grab our things, then us, to safety. No one said anything, but there was a bit of an atmosphere, and I think it was mutually understood that our crossing might have ended differently.

***

With winter work behind us, the long months of summer yawned ahead. Talking amongst friends, we met one or two other boats who were planning a trip to Brittany. Although it would be fun to sail in company, we almost always went alone. We don't like holding people up, and decisions about navigation always seem to be simpler when you only have to consider yourselves.

We set off without a word at sunrise on a morning, which promised a fine day ahead. Only the sea guessed our plan. We drifted past St Anthony's Head Lighthouse, which marks the entrance to the Fal Estuary, grey and colourless in the half light of dawn, said goodbye, promised to return in a few months, and then watched the sea quickly turn to indigo as we sailed into deep water. Even the swell was half-asleep, and heaved us gently over her furrows. The wind hadn't yet decided from which direction to blow – or even if it would blow at all – and filled the sails, now and then, with just enough wind to get us offshore before falling increasingly light, and then disappearing altogether. As time passed, and the sun climbed in the east, the wind sprang up from dead-ahead, then it arrived from different points astern, causing the boom to swing heavily first to one side, then to the other, whilst the sails slatted, irritatingly.

Linda was busy down below, but popped her head out from time to time to blink at the horizon as she dried her hair or brushed her teeth, lost in thought. The only sound was the creaking of our blocks every time we rolled over a wave which had just arrived from an unexpected direction, and headed off without knowing where it was supposed to be going. Our sail-cloth fidgeted, rearranging its lazy folds to a new breeze which would arrive and fail moments later. We were becalmed 2 miles into our 110-mile journey.

'If this wind doesn't pick up soon we might as well head back and try again tomorrow,' I said.

Linda was standing on the companionway steps, leaning on the coach-house roof, staring off into the distance, then swapping sides for a change of view, trance-like in the peace and quiet.

'Uh-huh,' was all she said.

Setting aside the fact that we were on passage to France – albeit not doing very well – it was just as pleasant, *more* so, simply to float around becalmed whilst the sun climbed in the morning sky, beaming down its cheerful rays.

'Shall we put the engine on?' I suggested.

'Could do,' Linda said in a voice which meant, *No*... 'Why don't you get your fishing rod out?' she suggested.

I cast a lure into the glassy water. In the distance a school of dolphins passed by on their journey to the Atlantic to do some fishing of their own – we heard their splash even at that distance – energetic and brimming with the joy of life.

A basking shark swam within a hundred metres of us on his way inshore – a black triangular dorsal fin followed by the menacing-looking pendulum swing of its tail (though basking sharks are completely harmless). A gull flew low over the water, beating its wings purposefully, eyes fixed ahead, as though it had prepared itself mentally for a long journey, and all alone. Jonathan Livingstone Seagull.

The sound of an arrow being shot into the water by an archer, which had startled me, turned out to be a gannet, plunging into the deep. Overhead two or three more wheeled around before banking suddenly and rolling into a steep dive. They disappeared underwater, bobbing to the surface several seconds later, each in turn, with a fish. A moment's rest, a shake, and they were off again, wings beating close to the water before gathering speed and soaring up into the air.

Cat's paws promised the arrival of a breeze, which always seemed to be 'over there', but eventually our sails filled late in the morning, the boat settled on her course, and our speed built to 2 knots. By lunchtime we were getting some miles under our belt, and sat down in the cockpit, eating crusty sticks of French bread, thickly buttered with a hot mackerel fillet, freshly caught, steaming its savour into the air.

'All you need is patience,' Joshua Slocum said, about his voyage around the world. I get frustrated by slow progress. Linda is more sanguine, but I'd turn back – if it didn't mean turning back.

During the afternoon the wind set in with a bit more purpose, taking us far offshore and then abandoning us for the night. We started the engine – Joshua Slocum didn't have an engine – and we droned through the darkness over the long swell for the next six hours. I was sure that my *Regulations for the Prevention of Collisions at Sea* forbade the exhibition of 'any other light than those prescribed', yet out there in the mid-channel shipping lanes it seemed as though late-night shopping arcades were being dragged over the horizon to tempt us. When we built our hollow wooden mast we crammed it full of aluminium pie dishes in a 50ft column, in lieu of a radar reflector. It gives an impressive radar echo, allowing us to punch above our weight, making us look bigger and more significant than we really are. Ship's captains, noticing a hell of a blip on their screens, narrow their eyes into the darkness where we are, yet see nothing at all – our pimple of a yacht light having gone unnoticed – and in their disconcertion steer several miles out of our way to be on the safe side. Usually.

When you peer at the rocks off the coast of France, you somehow know they are French. Whether it's because they smell of aftershave, or the climate that hangs over them has become a tad more Mediterranean, it's hard to say. The rocks here are as black as those in Cornwall, or Scotland – the sea as blue, the mist is as grey – but one glance at *these* rocks tells you that you are in France. 'Bienvenue,' they seem to say.

We skip French north coast harbours on our dazed arrival because of the lack of a distinct line between land and sea. Nameless chunks of France have broken off and litter the shore for a distance of two, sometimes three miles to seaward, as though the country was slowly fragmenting. Even Cowper in his *Sailing Tours* didn't advise the hardy corinthian to attempt them (though, of course, he himself made nothing of them). The tide here runs at up to 4 knots, pushing you to one side of your intended course – what was ahead a minute ago has exited off-stage left when you next look up. How much better for our tired minds, we reason, to turn our vessel slightly to the right, look out for that monstrosity of a light at Le Four, and with the tide going our way, we'll be swept around the north-west corner of France and onto the magic carpet that is the Chenal du Four in no time. And as for identifying where we are on the chart – why, as soon as you realise that these grotesque columns of concrete are in fact aids to navigation, you can be as certain of where you are as anyone who opens their curtains to gaze out on Didcot power station. We whoosh by, vowing to explore the north coast on the way back.

We always make Cameret-sur-Mer our port of arrival so we weren't astonished to find ourselves landing there again this time. As long as the wind hasn't got any north or east in it, Cameret is a comfortable harbour. If there *is* any north or east in the wind, the pontoon berths are protected by a wave-breaker – so we can be sure of a good night's sleep, whatever the weather. With the wind in the south west, and light, we anchored in the main harbour and found that the accommodation there was superior to the pontoons, because it was quieter. The smell of patisseries and the scented dust of the town wafted over the harbour.

First thing the next day we followed our noses, rowed ashore, and walked into town along a beach where a fit and tanned kitesurfer was struggling to get started – he was wearing a harness attached to a kite, which flew in lusty stunts – skimming the surface of the water before soaring up to the clouds. The surfer was leaning back against the pull of all this, trying to drag it back to his board – which was waiting on the sand a few yards behind him – and with each new struggle he lost more ground. He must have been trying for a while because he'd got four days' stubble.

In town we bought some sticky buns, and ate them virtually before we got to the door. Linda went for a good nose about the town whilst I sat on the beach to draw one of its wooden wrecks.

Linda is a scrupulous shopper; no premises remain un-browsed, regardless of in what tatty back-alley they may reside. As the hours rolled by I gradually lost my fear that someone would wander down the beach, look over my shoulder, and tell me that my scrawls were not commercial.

That evening we sat in the cockpit with a selection of cheeses and charcuterie, together with French sticks which were so long it was impractical to try to get them indoors, and which were quite dangerous in our amateur hands. After a herculean tug to break off an end, we'd look up in triumph only to find we'd put the other person's eye out.

It was just like Christmas, this 'shopping in a foreign country' – bringing everything home and then unwrapping all the parcels to see what you'd got. Linda had bought some of that cheese which smells like a rat that's died behind the radiator so I had to sit upwind of her when she opened that one. She'd also got some saucisson which I grudgingly admitted wasn't as bad as the one she'd bought a couple of years previously, and which

Nothing stirs

she'd carried home followed by a cloud of blue-bottles. When she offered me a slice of this one, with her mouth full and a smile from ear to ear, even I was forced to concede that it smelt and tasted no worse than a mummified corpse. Everything seemed to go so well with the soft red wine she'd chosen and at such a good price that one bottle was hardly enough. Each.

The reason French meals go on for hours is that they take so much chewing, and whilst we were thus employed, working our jaws and scanning our new environment for some visual distraction, we were astonished by the appearance from seaward of a huge schooner, turning as slowly as a planet as it entered the harbour and flying the Stars and Stripes on a piece of cloth the size of a rain cover for the centre court at Wimbledon. This schooner was a larger version of the one we'd encountered at Dartmouth and provided employment for twenty men above decks, all dressed in white tunics and hats like the makers of award-winning hamburgers. The vessel pointed its bowsprit at us and came in. When it became clear that he intended to anchor alongside, I wondered if it was in retaliation for the Dartmouth incident.

My manual of seamanship lays down a rule-of-thumb for setting anchors: multiply the depth at HW by three (four if there's much of a breeze) and pay out that amount of chain. Depth 10 metres; out goes 30–40 metres of chain. The owner of the schooner had read the same manual, but for some romantic reason his anchor was attached, not to chain, but to rope as thick as your thigh. The rule is different for rope – the rule-of-thumb there is that you lay out 10 times the depth. Depth 10 metres; out goes 100 metres of rope. Our boat lay anchored amongst a small flotilla of about twenty other craft. If the schooner had chosen to anchor at the back of all of us, he would have drifted downwind and away by a further 100 metres to the entire satisfaction of everyone, who, having got here first were, like us, watching developments whilst they industriously chewed their baguettes. But the Stars and Stripes should never be seen at the back of a fleet, the owner felt; so he dropped his anchor at the head of the fleet, and chucked out 100 metres of plaited rope behind it. I'll never forget the look of bafflement and disappointment on the face of the owner as his craft drifted back through the fleet – knit one, pearl one – until his rope cable was stretched and he brought up somewhere about the middle of us. He leant over the varnished cherry of his handrail and looked down on us all, appalled, as a tourist does when the coach he's on is being driven through the slums.

We all watched, yet none durst ask him if he thought it was gonna fly.

Against my expectations, that night was undisturbed; the trouble only began at 6am the following morning when the schooner went to leave to meet an appointment his wife had made to have her hair done in Bordeaux. All his attempts to retrieve his anchor were thwarted: deep underwater on the seabed the rope had found its way around every plastic chair, ship's cannon and scrapped 2CV in the harbour, not to mention the flukes of all our anchors. For two hours they struggled, gaining a foot here and an old tyre there, until by eight o'clock they'd retrieved nearly a yard of rope back on board. The captain of the schooner lined his crew along the side-deck for a little chat. It must have been very constructive because as the meeting drew to a close he pointed a finger at one of them, and in New York office drawl told him: 'I agree with your analysis.'

Ever since then, whenever Linda and I are mid-disaster, clutching at straws, and one of us makes a futile suggestion about how we got into the mess in the first place, we agree with the other's analysis.

At ten, a local team of divers in dry suits motored out to the schooner and rolled over the side of their RIB to unpick his knitting. Half an hour later the vessel egressed regally from port, Stars and Stripes fluttering.

Elsewhere in port, parting laughter rang out from the pontoons bringing our attention to where a yacht was just leaving, towing an inflatable dinghy in a novel manner. They were packed in like sardines over there and there was no room, it seems, for the dinghy to float free. So the parting yachtsman had hit upon the clever idea of leaving his dinghy high and dry on the pontoon, and allowing his yacht to pluck it into the water behind him as he motored away. Things weren't going according to plan. The dinghy's painter had snagged under a mooring cleat, effectively securing the yacht, as it tried to get away, by the stern. Increasing the throttle only stretched the rubber dinghy to an odd shape. Then the wind took charge and blew him backwards until he collided with the boats behind him. Shrieks rang out, people rushed around holding fenders on bits of string, helpful suggestions were bellowed out to anyone who would listen. Situations like these are always accompanied by a good deal of yelling – just so no one the other side of the harbour misses the fun. We watched through the binoculars with the usual mix of amusement, and relief. I found it gratifying that I'm not alone in my willingness to make a complete ass of myself for the entertainment of others.

People in the know say that the climate changes as soon as you go round the Raz de Sein – for the better, if you happen to be going south. Perhaps it really does or perhaps it's just that your mood lifts, having survived another navigational hazard. We've noticed a similar phenomenon ashore: our moods lift when we're driving from Scotland to the south coast of England and we clear the dangers of Birmingham.

We basted ourselves in coconut oil now that our bodies were exposed to the full glow of a blinding-hot sun, reflected by the white-sand beaches. Sunglasses which had seemed more-than-adequate in Scotland struggled to cope even though I'd painted the lenses with black gloss. And the suntan lotion might as well have been lard when we saw how prawn-pink we were at the end of the day.

Ashore at Audierne there was a change in the *social* atmosphere, too. Everyone except the gendarmes drifted about in colourful beach attire and holiday smiles. Linda took to wearing a broad-brimmed straw hat with a pink scarf tied around it and looked just like a native. I walked past her twice without recognising her.

Shops round here only stocked fritteries and prices rocketed. At night the town of Audierne pulsed pink and blue lights out to us – in a tasteful way – over the mirrored surface of the water. Wavelets could be heard curling over on the sandy beach with a soft hush, and no one to see them. The sound of music and laughter drifted out to us. All seemed strange, exotic and new, but below our feet the boards of our boat, as familiar as two thousand nights aboard could make her, was ready to take us where we wanted to go, yet bringing with her all the familiar things of home. The anchorage at Audierne is quite exposed and rolly. So we stayed just one night.

In the entrance to the River Odet late the following afternoon – just as day-trippers-by-boat were returning to their moorings from a tediously slow day on the nature reserve 'Iles de Glenan' – a great lump of a 'stink boat' boat came flying past at a speed and distance which really was reckless, and left us in a cloud of black smoke. I don't know if they rocket past to show us how slow we are or whether they want a close look at how beautiful we are or it's just that we happen to be on the straight-line course between where they've come from and where they're going, but we seem to attract more than our fair share of close-passes from bronzed lunatics with gold medallions nestling in their grey chest hair.

He slowed rapidly once he'd passed us – leaving us slewing in his wake – then he appeared on deck with a camera (*his* deck, I mean).

'Allo! Allo!' He waved, as though we hadn't noticed him yet, then lifted his camera to indicate to us that we should pose. Confidentially I was still bristling a little bit. I didn't even let him have my best side.

When the photo-shoot was over, he yelled, 'What is your email? I send you.'

He yelled an instruction up to the steering position. Whether he'd transferred command of his vessel to an idiot-brother, a child of five or just left it to its own devices we couldn't see because the conning tower was so high, but one minute he was standing 50 metres away with a pencil and paper in his hand, and the next his bow arrived overhead as though it meant to mount us. I called out my email address, knowing that the photo would never arrive because even the English have trouble spelling Tyers.

'OK – I send. I send. Very byootifool! Sank you!'

With that he zoomed off, leaving us in more diesel smoke. It was several minutes before it lifted enough to allow us to see the harbour for which we were heading, but he could charm the birds out of a tree, that man, because when he'd gone I remarked to Linda what a nice boat he had.

I like to walk through woodland, Linda likes to walk through towns, so there is always a compromise to be struck about where we moor. Though thankfully Linda is prepared to walk *through* woodland to get to a town. We dropped anchor in a little creek, by a wood, which had a path leading to a small hamlet – it was so pastoral that even the water in which we floated was lime-green. This was the kind of creek into which, historically, old boats at the end of their lives were towed to their 'retirement' – three of them lay submerged in mud even now at its head waters. These old wooden boats were hugely overbuilt, using great baulks of timber fit for the rugged work they performed in all weather at sea. Those boats which were not lost in storms might give a hundred years' service before eventually being replaced. Even now the boats laid up here had refused to rot and crumble.

The French goverment hold the greatest collection of maritime history in the world, and keeps it scattered about at the tops of rivers where no one goes. When you lay your hand on the joinery you connect yourself with the hand of the craftsman who fashioned it, and answer him the question most on his mind at the time. For how long will I be immortalised by my work? How far will my effort reach into the future? And what will be its fate? And you hear the shouts of the generations of men who succeeded him and worked the boat during its long life. In the creek before us lay a boat so complete that we almost imagined she could sail again, if only her missing boards were replaced. Alongside her, another wreck – her back broken and her boards sprung – and in between the two, we almost forgot to notice a much older vessel. She may have sailed during the French Revolution, and been lying here when these newcomers were being built. Of her only a board or two remained above the mud to fire the imagination with stirring tales from those romantic days when lives at sea were hard and short.

The foredeck of an ancient craft

On passage to the Morbihan, there are several islands which make a great stopover. That's irresponsible talk from voyagers who have only tried two of them – Belle-Ile and Houat – but they all seem the sort of places where artists go 'for the light'. White sands and a turquoise sea give the islands an incandescent quality and it's hard to visit any small island during the summer months and not feel as though you're laying down some memories for life. If we had to award a 'first-place' of the two we've tried, it would have to be Houat because the ice cream was so nice.

Pilots and Almanacs tend to overstate the difficulties you'll face when visiting certain places – after all, they can't know on which day you intend to visit, and what the sea and weather conditions will be like *at that time*, so they cover themselves by dealing with a worst case scenario. But mere words can't prepare you for the entrance to the Morbihan on a good day. As soon as you get there you know you are dealing with something capricious and unpredictable. At its entrance there is no question of stemming the tide, which runs at up to 10 knots. We came in – like everyone else – with the tide in our favour, threw ourselves at its mercy, and watched the shore pass us as spectators. Inside, if all went well, we'd decided which bit of the Morbihan we'd like to visit as 'first choice', and then picked another, further in, as second choice – just in case we got washed past the first one before we had a chance to hook it with our anchor.

The Gulf of Morbihan is an inland sea about ten miles wide and four high, though that's just rough because bits of it go off in all directions. It's littered with pretty islands, mostly private, but we felt we could spend a summer in the Morbihan and park somewhere new every night around the shores of those islands, taking refuge in tidal eddies which never sleep.

Three miles from the entrance we threw our anchor into a mere 2 knots of tide, breathed a sigh of relief, and settled back to admire a small herd of *vaches* which were grazing a few yards from our bowsprit. We were feeling rather pleased with ourselves, actually, because this was the bit we were aiming for. We rowed into the tributary, which was too shallow for the 'big boat', and discovered that it, together with its tall houses planted high on the river banks, were part of an old industry – oysters have been farmed intensively hereabouts for 200 years (and probably much longer) – as witnessed by the stacks of fluted ceramic tiles, now covered in calcium deposits, which had been laid to seed the oyster 'spat'. Mountains of tiles had been gathered up and stacked to form great walls along the river bank, overgrown now with bramble, yet many more had been abandoned in situ and littered the seabed, leaving odd ruddy corners of clay peeping up through the mud and shingle. A road bridge carrying hurtling traffic overflew the wet mud of the estuary, emphasising that all below it had been superseded, and belonged to the past.

Our next excursion – when we'd already been in the Morbihan for several days and felt we knew the place like locals – took us from one side of the divided entrance to the other. The geography meant we had to force ourselves upstream through the white-water rapids of the fill-water, tumbling over itself with excitement near the narrow entrance, before turning left around a beacon which marked a shingly beach, where at last we could go with the flow. Things seemed to be going quite well as we bucked and reared toward the entrance, so I allowed myself a moment to smile into the sunlit sky and noticed to my astonishment that our masthead light had detached itself from its mounting and was now dangling by its electric cable, banging against the mast like a medieval lantern-on-a-stick. It was only a matter of time before it would smash itself into a thousand plastic pieces, yet if it could hold on, and I could get to it first, I'd save myself £120. I'm not one of those who can open their wallet and whistle a merry tune at the same time so beads of sweat gathered on my brow.

In fact, the sight of it banging about up there so fascinated my mind that I entered a sort of time-warp, and the next time I looked to my ship we were about to beach ourselves on the shingle at the foot of the largest beacon in the Morbihan, which I swear had been half a mile away only moments earlier. As I swung away I could see every stone on that beach, and because we were in the grip of the tide, I was getting a closer look with every second that passed. I slammed the control lever to full throttle just as the stern rose to a sort of 'bow' wave that surrounded the beacon, metres off its shore. Linda doesn't like it when the engine is run at full throttle – experience has taught her that *bad* things happen at full throttle. She turned to face me from her station on the foredeck, and I could see her mouth opening and closing urgently. But at full revs our under-felt is no match for the engine noise, and the information she wished to put me in possession of was lost.

We inched back on course and then shot around the corner. Whole islands flew past, left and right, and when I couldn't identify them fast enough from the chart, I abandoned that, and followed the boat ahead, who seemed to know what he was doing. Several miles later, in a new world where no one would recognise us, we slipped into an eddying backwater, drifted into the shallows over white sand, and threw out the anchor. I adopt a completely different work ethic at the top of the mast – instead of applying my usual standards, best characterised as 'botch and go', atop the mast I strive for quality of workmanship in the certain knowledge that it will increase the number of days between this sickening trip and the next time I'll have to be up here. I reattached the light to its masthead and it is unlikely that the two could now be separated by an explosives expert.

We found uncluttered anchorages. By day we landed and explored, and by night we sat in the cockpit on timber boards that shone lustrously from spillages of olive oil and anchovy. We heard the easy laughter of people eating on terraces under the shade of vines, and an air of luxurious contentment hung over the region.

We braced ourselves for a visit to Vannes. It's easily the biggest town on the many and convoluted shores of the Morbihan and we'd waited for our visit to coincide with that moment when our cupboards were bare. From the descriptions we'd heard, Vannes would come as a shock to our senses after our long sojourn in idyllic tranquillity.

When we arrived in the early afternoon its fish market was doing a thriving trade. There was a bottleneck at the entrance to the drab building. Many thousands of French people who hadn't bought a fish yet were trying to get in. It's one of the differences between the English and French culture that in England, fish counters – say in a supermarket – are deserted; they are merely a statement that this retailer believes in offering its customers really fresh produce. Crikey, if it wasn't for the smell of rotting fish no one would notice it was there! The only visitors to a fish counter in England are boys wearing school shorts who have to come to prod the wet corpses with a finger.

Here at the fish market in Vannes the mood was becoming angry – people who *had* bought a fish were trying to get out with it but found themselves lifted bodily off the ground, only to be carried back into the building by the crush. Linda and I had no intention of visiting the fish market at all as we passed by, but our sympathies were aroused by the anxiety of the crowd. At first we only took the part of the weak and the vulnerable, helping them by pushing them from the back in the hope of advancing their progress through the mob, yet before long we were caught up emotionally in the frenzied mood, and at a signal threw ourselves bodily over their heads, desperately clawing our way to the front and elbowing all who tried to stop us.

French people prefer, and are willing to pay for, food that has grown up wild and been landed fresh that morning. Inside we wandered past countless stalls in the tiled hall, down its aisle-ways, past stainless steel trays displaying mounds of dead fish. The winkles – which were alive and have been speed-limited by nature not to exceed 1 mile per year, during which time they *must* find a dead fish – couldn't believe their luck.

Even in my fascinated distraction, as I examined all the different species I noticed that there was a bit of a commotion behind me – a murmur from the crowd as though some dignitary had just walked in. I didn't turn round to see who it was because I never recognise famous people in my *own* country but I was *aware* of it. For the next couple of minutes the famous person shadowed me. Wherever I went, he followed, and was beginning to cause such a stir that a void had built up around me which no one dare enter as a mark of respect. At last I turned to take a look at the important personage, only to be met by hundreds of pairs of eyes staring back at me – shoppers and stallholders alike – smiling, and nodding at me with knowing looks. I checked my flies.

Suddenly a stallholder climbed onto a fish crate and called out, 'Beel Clinton.'

That seemed to confirm the thought on everyone's mind, and a great assent passed through the lips of the crowd. Taking the joke in good part I smiled back at them. That clinched it.

'Beel Clinton – monsieur le president,' I heard them informing each other.

Undecided between disappointing them, or offering to sign a treaty, I chose the middle way and carried on browsing, but whereas moments earlier I'd been forced to struggle through the crowd, I now found that whichever way I turned a path was cleared before me and all that was expected of me was to step, statesmanlike, into it.

The admiration of a crowd is very elevating. It changed the way I walk. I was just swaggering past a row of fine-looking turbot with my hands clasped behind my back, when I learned the second lesson fame teaches you – how shallow and fickle people are. I noticed that my public had grown tired of me and that the darling of their attention now was *Linda* – who under no circumstances could be mistaken for Hillary. 'She must be his new secretary...' you could hear people saying, 'Come along to help Bill lick his stamps...' And they gazed at her, drinking in an impression of her face to know what a philatelist looked like. When they glanced back at me, it was simply to lift their eyebrows once, and to nod, by way of letting me know that they had the whole story.

We did what British people usually do in a fish market – looked at all the fish, pursed our lips at the prices, and then left in search of a butcher. We'd got a bee in our bonnet about Poulet Noir. By then it was getting late in the day and the only produce that remained amid the chaos of half-dismantled market stalls was the outer leaves of cabbages and the green tops of carrots trodden into the cobbled streets. We spotted a boucher who had decided to give it 'five more minutes'. All he had left were the pigs' trotters his dog couldn't manage, and the emaciated corpses of two birds, which I took to be a mating pair of starlings the butcher had found in a bricked-up chimney he'd knocked through to open up the fireplace. He'd just let out a long sigh of despair and hauled himself off the countertop in preparation for going home when he noticed that we'd stopped in front of his stall. There was a sudden burst of knife sharpening.

'Bon après midi!' Linda said, clearing up any doubt he may have had that we were English. 'Avez-vous une Poulet Noir?'

He pointed to the starlings.

'Bien sûr! Mais voila!' Linda asked him to price the larger of the two. With the exception of its mate, it was the scrawniest looking wretch you have ever seen. It was heart-breaking to think how it must have fluttered about the chimney before starving to death. Monsieur le Boucher weighed it, adjusted the €/Kg dial up to the top of its range, and sold it to us as Wagyu

Steak. Back on board, with the beast cooked on our plates before us, we were surprised to find that starling smells a lot like chicken – after all, not all chicken smells like chicken. But in the fantasy world of our imaginations we'd assumed you got some meat on a Poulet Noir. Examining what was before us, leaving no bone unturned, there wasn't a morsel to eat.

Vannes wasn't our favourite stop. The marina is right in the centre of the town, which is a novelty, but just as pitching your tent on a city centre roundabout seems like an amusing idea at first, the experience of being afloat amid urban sprawl soon poisons the spirit. The noise; the fumes from exhaust pipes reversing into parking spaces just above your head, the sense of being watched by hundreds of pairs of eyes, which follow you every time you step on deck, takes more away from you than it gives back.

After a couple of days we decided to leave, which entailed passing back along the narrow canalled section of waterway and out into the Morbihan via a sea-gate which is only opened for an hour or so either side of high water. As the tide outside rises, and the grand opening-of-the-gate becomes imminent, there is a terrible firing up of marine engines, shouts as lines are released and chucked through the air, black clouds of smoke mushroom out from the backs of boats, and there is a scramble for the gate because if you miss it, it won't open again until tomorrow, and you're forced to enjoy another day in Vannes.

What we thought was meant to happen was that you paid for your mooring as you went back out through the gate, because unless I'm mistaken I think we were given our ticket when we passed through it on our way *in*. I confess right now that some friends of ours with whom we arrived, and with whom we were now leaving, mentioned that we should have *already* paid for our mooring at a little office in the town. But since you had to walk round the whole marina to get to the ticket office, and time was short – there was already a queue to get into the canal – we decided to slip our lines and do a runner. All went well until we slowed down in the vicinity of the gate. A dory with writing on the side came powering up to the stern of each yacht in the queue and called the vessel's name into a handheld VHF radio, grassing them up to 'mission control'. The girl in the dory came to our stern and announced us into her lapel.

'Kah ol eela,' she said.

That's all right, I remember thinking, *they'll never work it out from that.* There followed a long silence whilst records were being checked and the guiltless smiles we wore began to strain. At last the radio burst into life, once more asking for clarification – in French, of course.

She read our name board again: 'C-A-O-L I-L-A,' she said, spelling it out letter by letter.

Then we heard a rapid exchange of information between the two of them as though they were dealing with a live and fast-developing situation. Although we didn't understand the actual words being said there could be no mistaking that things were turning *très sérieux* by the tone of what was going on. Weighty decisions were being made concerning our future which, once settled, would be irreversible. Would they distrain our vessel, I began to wonder? But no – they were very polite and, dealing with us as though we had merely *forgotten* – oh la la – to pay our harbour dues, handed us a bill for quite a surprising amount of money – but there, what price can you put on memories?

By August the weather begins to change. In the morning we climb the companionway steps to see what the new day has brought and look across dewy decks, out onto the hanging mists. Time to make some decisions about the coming winter: where do we want to be, where will we find work, and from what woods will we glean our winter fuel?

Not being long-distance, hot-climate people, Cornwall offers familiarity, and mild winters. We know where to find protection in the angles of its rivers. We know where to find the rare or unusual requisites of life aboard in its towns – towns which have been serving the maritime community for hundreds of years, and as we walk its streets we see the familiar faces of people who are not astounded to notice how unfashionably we dress, nor mind our rosy outdoor faces, or the smell of wood-smoke in our hair. We wonder if we might stay in France – try it for a winter – but we never do.

By the time we got back to the north coast of France the fogs of September were rolling into the Channel. We tucked ourselves upriver in L'Aber Benoît – across from Falmouth, but separated by the English Channel and a hundred miles of sea. We picked up a large private mooring, cloistered from danger, heard no objections, and waited for a change in the forecast. Early in the morning a day or two later a hail brought us on deck – friends of ours from Falmouth who we didn't realise were in port were leaving to cross the Channel, knew we didn't carry a radar and offered to pilot us through the fog. It was tempting, but we knew that they were planning to make the crossing at 8 knots, whereas we prefer 5. In our minds cruising at 5 knots saves straining the engine, and the boat, though we're probably wrong about that. We didn't want to hold them back, thanked them, and dolefully watched them motor out of the harbour, and become absorbed by the fog.

In L'Aber Wrach, a village nearby, we'd noticed a very smart-looking restaurant and decided to cheer ourselves up with one last unforgettable meal. At the reception desk, an haute-coutured dazzlingly attractive woman in her thirties with a welcoming smile sang out a greeting: 'Bon soir!'

We'd picked up some French: 'On peut manger?' we asked.

I'm quite a good mimic and when those four syllables rolled off my tongue, you couldn't tell them from the real thing. In her quick-fire reply I picked up the word 'reservation' and she began scouring a sheet of paper with a list of names on it. Putting two and two together I deduced that we should have booked for any chance of sampling their bon bouches.

We crossed the road to look at a menu hanging in the window of a neon-lit eatery then carried on walking when two children emerged from it carrying French sticks slashed along one edge and overfilled with chips. We slipped into the only other restaurant in town no-questions-asked and didn't notice until we'd sat down that we were the only diners. But the crusty bread with Normandy butter, plump moist steaks and crisp salads were so bursting with flavour and texture we wondered if fate might have played a hand, and not only that but we were served by cheerful staff who *intended* us to have a nice evening, which I think contributes more to a meal than the food, or as much as.

A few days later, when the visibility improved, we slid downriver past trots of moorings, watched the green banks littered with the white dots of immaculate bungalows drift into our history, and picked our way through the littering of rocks and shoals, out to sea. The wind, very conveniently, was on the port quarter, our sails and rigging came taut. *Caol Ila* hauled herself over the first wave, hushing a little foam in its trough and seemed to sigh: *Right then, be patient, relax, and I'll take you home.*

For the next 24 hours we rode the swell, gently rolling over identical waves, sinking into each trough with a hush of foam, watching our wake quietly spinning out astern. Linda and I don't speak much when we're on passage. We catch each other's eyes to see how we're doing. We scan the (usually) empty horizon frequently, mark the passage of hours with regular meals, snacks and hot drinks, divide the night into two-hour watches, and spend the hours of darkness just as we spend the day – with our backs toward the wind, snugged up in all-weather gear, helming our boat over the restless sea. During the day, if there are clouds, we steer by them; at night, if there are stars we steer to those, dropping our heads to check our course occasionally against the lubber line of our compass. Nothing else occupies us. We are in suspended animation.

Every so often a fulmar drops by to see what we are. Like bumblebees their shape isn't ideally suited to flight and they seem to make heavy weather of it, each wing-beat coming just in time to save them. They circle us once, turning their heads over their shoulders, frequently looking us full in the eyes, and seem to wonder at our odd way of getting about. Arriving at night they are illuminated by our navigation lights, changing from red to white to green as they circle us. Then they're gone.

Near dawn a light flashed ahead, once – just the loom of it seen on the underside of some low clouds, staring into that quarter we didn't see it again. Nevertheless we knew it was there, and suspicions rose that in another mile or two it would resolve itself into the lighthouse at Lizard Point – the most southerly point of Britain, and the first glimpse we would get of home, visual confirmation of where we were. The music returned to our voices, excited by the expectation of familiar sights. Our hearts leaped with joy to see our old friends: the black rocks sprinkled like crumbs of burnt toast in the sea off Lizard Point, its lighthouse – serving only us – perched on the clifftop. We began to chatter, making up for our day of silence.

'Looks a bit rough over there...'

'Wind over tide, I expect.'

'Be calmer by nine.'

'Won't matter to us – we're not going through it.'

Close inshore, in the full light of early morning, along a stretch of coast with no obvious harbours, open boats busily work the lonely rocks. Two long bamboo canes, each reaching far out to one side, trail bass lures through the smooth water amongst rocks. When a fish strikes, the rod swings aft, and the fisherman knows he has a bite. It's not industrial fishing, it's proper sustainable fishing unchanged in generations, carried out by Celtic Cornishmen whose cottages hide in coves which are easier to get to by boat than car.

A couple of hours later we passed through the entrance to the Fal, so familiar to us now that it felt like home. Perhaps it is home, though we can't always be there. It's certainly home to the Falmouth Pilot Cutter, so our boat feels at home.

The end of the summer is a time for catching up with boaty friends to hear what they've been up to and swap disaster stories, so a day or two later we arranged a beach barbecue, to which everyone brought a big fat steak. We found a spot protected from the wind by a hillock, treed with oak, gathered together enough firewood for a County bonfire, and sat next to its crackling flames in the soft dusk. A welcome orange glow surrounded us, lighting the branches above our heads.

Marc and Anne phoned. They were running late sailing back from Plymouth, the wind had died, they'd just come round St Anthony's Head and were churning hard to 'be there

Up the creek

in an hour'. No problem, the flames of the fire were at their height – cooking is more controllable when the flames have died down to leave a deep bed of fiercely glowing embers. I once set an aluminium pan – half filled with oil for frying chips – onto a camp fire which was flaming heroically, and then distantly heard the phone ring. This was back in the days when we lived in a house. I ran to answer the phone, had a conversation with whoever it was, fiddled about, then suddenly remembered my pan. By the time I got back to the fire I was expecting to see my pan well-alight but instead, there was nothing – no pan because Linda had taken it off... or so I imagined. I sat down on an upturned log next-the-fire, wondering where she'd put the pan, when it suddenly dawned on me that Linda wasn't even home yet. Then, on the ground under and around the burning sticks of the fire, something shiny caught my eye, and a moment later I realised that it was a pool of molten aluminium – all that was left of my pan.

Back in Cornwall, we sat on logs around the fire, laughing, and wafting away the sweet smoke whenever it came our way. We drank wine, and salivated in anticipation of the eight fillet steaks which formed a tall stack, wrapped in greaseproof paper. Before we knew five minutes had slipped by, we heard an anchor chain rattle into the water just around the corner and moments later Marc and Anne rowed into view, smiling and fresh from their travels.

I've heard you can buy the most amazing oven chips these days, where you just need to shine a torch on the packet and they're done, but we cut ours from the tubers of real potatoes, patted them dry on tea towels, and then fried them – twice. The first frying to cook them, without letting them go brown. The second frying – moments before they were to be served – crisped them, and turned them golden brown. It was embarrassing how good they tasted.

The blue cheese sauce (sweated onions and garlic, Stilton, single cream) had bubbled to perfection. I took orders for how everyone would like their steaks 'done', lubricated the meat by dipping each one into lukewarm beef-dripping, and then threw them onto a wire rack placed just above the scalding embers. The dripping fat set an inferno going there that moments later consumed our steaks in flame. Shocked laughter rang out as hungry diners watched £60 of prime beef incinerate. Even I had misgivings when the flames went above my head but held my nerve – just – and stuck to the timings, then served each diner according to his or her preference of 'doneness'. You could cut those steaks with a butter-knife, and once cut, pink juices oozed for those who like pink juices, and didn't for those who don't. No one could be persuaded to swap his or her steak for one lesser done, nor to have theirs cooked a moment longer, and for a quarter of an hour afterwards the only words to leave anyone's lips were 'Mmm!', 'God!' and 'Wow!'

Don had been a banker and I'm sure he earned good money in the rich-but-dangerous diamond-mining area of South Africa. He must have had a few prime steaks in his time, and he was the first to say anything coherent.

'That was the best steak I've ever eaten!' he chuckled as we all mopped up the juices on our plates, kicked back, and then settled to enjoy the warmth of the fire.

Don told us about the first boat he ever bought – a dinghy and trailer which he and his wife Penny picked up in Surrey to tow to the coast. Don is easy to listen to, and doesn't mind telling a story against himself. He didn't know anything about boats – he said – but it was only when he came to pick his new boat up that he realised he didn't know anything about trailers either.

'How's this go?' he said to Penny as he fumbled with the tow ball and hitch. When he thought it was 'all right', they set off, making allowance for the increased length of his vehicle by taking the long line around corners. For a while everything seemed to go quite well. Then he described how he was driving along when he happened to look out of his side window and noticed that they were being overtaken by a trailer. He thought it a bit strange but said nothing until it had overtaken them. Then he recognised it.

'That's *our* trailer!'

'Gosh!'

'What shall we do?' he said.

'Let's follow it!'

The trailer ran for a hundred yards before veering across the carriageway and into the drive of a house where a BMW and a Mercedes were parked. Shooting between the two, it only came to a stop when it hit the wall of the house. The owner, who happened to be standing in the garden, watched it arrive. Don and Penny got out of their car full of apologies.

'Nothing like this has ever happened to me before...'

The owner shrugged. 'Don't worry about it – things like this seem to happen all the time here. We put it down to the fact that our house is number 13.'

When the embers of the fire had dwindled to a dull glow, the wine had all been drunk and with the tide falling, we carried our dinghies over the slippery weed to the water's edge, climbed in, and paddled reluctantly home, laughter still ringing out over the water.

A day or two later I went to the library in Falmouth with the intention of emptying my email inbox after the long summer. My email client pinged into life, and my emails formed an orderly queue on the page. There were four. One of them was from someone I didn't know in France and had an attachment – a photograph of our boat. I know it's supposed to be very flattering when someone takes a photo of your boat and sends it to you, but it struck me that this was some kind of joke. I didn't recognise the person standing on our deck, and couldn't remember having invited him on board, so it seemed that someone had got onto our boat in our absence and had a photograph of themselves taken looking very proprietorial on the foredeck: a fat bloke gurning up at the camera as though he owned the bloody thing – not only that but he was topless, wearing only a pair of shorts under his big belly, which, being old-fashioned, I thought disrespectful.

I pushed my head toward the screen and looked narrowly at the photograph, observing its surroundings in an attempt to jog my memory. A glimmer of recognition stirred in my brain – his face began to ring a bell – then, with a jolt, I realised that he was me.

The river is quiet in early September when everyone has gone back to school, but suddenly jumps back to life for one last spasm on the second weekend for the *Last Night of the Proms*. The leafy upriver pontoon – where you can hear a bird yawning at a distance of half a mile – is the venue of a middle-aged rave. Fifty boats rush to tie alongside during the morning and afternoon, each reserving places for those who haven't yet arrived. Boomboxes are placed at strategic intervals and tuned into Radio 2. After dark, revellers tumble out of their boats, wearing dinner jackets and ball gowns, carrying plastic stemmed flutes filled with prosecco, and start waltzing along the pontoon to the acceptable face of classical music: *Sailing* by Rod Stewart (without the words), Beatles hits performed on the violin, and Acker Bilk's *Strangers on the Shore*.

The shocked silence of Sunday morning was broken by a jogging club at 8am for women in lycra. The pontoon is only a hundred yards long so to get a decent jog out of it you have to do, say, fifty lengths – all of which makes a noise like a lorry-load of steel drums that has been emptied down a rocky hill in an attempt to mask the sounds of a prison riot. Because we were only bystanders, looking in from the outside, and not caught up in the zone, we couldn't help getting anthropological and wondering where we're all headed, you know – as a species.

By Sunday evening the pontoon was clear. There'll only be one or two visitors between now and next April.

The days grew shorter; autumn gales blowing overhead were interspersed with days bathed in golden sunlight in which we owned the gliding river: we'd walk, shop, gather firewood, or visit friends. If it was dull, we'd mooch contentedly on board, cooking, drawing, reading or making lists for future plans. But the future isn't ours to mould and increasingly we spent time travelling up to Scotland because Linda's mum wasn't very well. When she didn't improve we decided we'd settle in Scotland for a while, find work, rent a house, and bring the boat up in the spring.

15 A HOME IN THE HEBRIDES

I'VE MENTIONED IT BEFORE, and I'll just mention it again, that donkey's years ago when I was living in London I drove 550 miles to Inverness on business. It was my first trip to Scotland. Before heading home I walked into a wine merchant and asked the chap behind the counter – whose beard was made of reds and browns which exactly matched the yarn in his Harris Tweed jacket – if he could recommend a whisky for me to take home. Without a word he turned, took a bottle from the shelf behind him, wrapped it in crepe paper, and placed it heavily on the counter in front of me.

'Try that,' he said.

As he handed me my change he gave me a look as though he knew he'd just changed my life for ever. Later, I unwrapped the bottle. Caol Ila. I couldn't even say it. Pronounced 'cull-eela', the label said, helpfully. Port Askaig, Isle of Islay.

It was that first acquaintance with the name Caol Ila which eventually led to our naming our boat *Caol Ila*, because Linda thought it sounded pretty. And it was that trip to Inverness all those years ago which suddenly began to shape our future once more: now that we wanted to be nearer to Linda's mum, and Linda was searching the NHS jobs database for work in Scotland, a job matching her qualifications came up on the Isle of Islay. She applied for and got the job. It wasn't practical to continue living on board if we were going to work for a living, so we asked around to see if there was a house available to rent on the island, and heard that there was. It was just uphill from the Caol Ila distillery.

I had a strange feeling of importance the following summer, arriving by boat to live on Islay. I motored into Port Ellen and tied up to the pontoons which everyone else was only visiting, put the kettle on, and then gazed out on the sights and sounds, thinking: *this is our new home.* Heavy showers – sudden and short lived – were the forerunners to an expected change in weather, and forced me back down below, pulling the hatch behind me.

Linda was arriving on Islay separately. She'd sailed up the coast of Ireland with me when, two days earlier, a forecast of strong northerlies made it look doubtful that we could arrive on Islay for a week. She was due to start work on Monday and because of bad weather earlier in the trip had already postponed her start date twice, so she set out on public transport from Strangford Lough in Northern Ireland. It took her two days, three buses, two trains and two ferries to get to Islay. In the event the 'strong northerlies' which had been forecast had been postponed too, and I'd continued the journey alone, arriving at Islay two hours before Linda's ferry was due. She and I had spoken on the phone, but I'd lied and hadn't told her that I'd carried on the journey and was already there. The ferry berth is just a few metres from the yachting pontoon so I watched through the binoculars as her ferry pulled in, saw her scanning the pontoon knowledgeably, and then watched her facial expressions as she spotted her own boat. I hid in a doorway as she got off the ferry. She pretended not to see me as she passed-by, but then suddenly swung her bag into my chest.

'And you can just carry that!' she said, knocking me backwards.

'Welcome to Islay,' I said.

'It's not funny!' she said, unable to stop herself from giggling.

Back on board later that afternoon I spotted a scallop dredger berthing alongside the dock and asked Linda if she'd mind popping along to ask if we could buy some scallops straight from the boat.

'Why don't you ask him yourself?'

'It's better coming from a woman.'

She rolled her eyes in exasperation then returned to what she was doing. After a minute or two I heard her swallow, and knew that in her mind's eye she could see a sizzling plate of seared scallops, drizzled with garlic and olive oil. A moment later she grabbed her handbag.

'Which boat did you say it was, anyway?'

Through the binoculars I saw the conversation between her and the fisherman, but my heart sank when I saw her turn back for home empty-handed.

'Any joy?'

'He hasn't got any left... What a lovely accent the islanders have.' By way of demonstrating it, she told me what he'd said, 'Och, everything's just this minute away on the van... but see if you're here tomorrow will I put some back for you?'

'Yes, please put some back.'

'How many woss you wantin?'

'Just enough for two...'

The following day when we saw the black booms of his dredger round the pier-head and slide into his usual berth, Linda hopped out to meet him, and I pressed the binoculars to my face once more. The skipper seemed to be looking out for Linda. When he saw her walk along the dock he leapt to the shore and pressed a bag into her hand. I couldn't help but let out a triumphant little 'Yes!'

I began peeling some garlic. I heard Linda's light footfall on deck, the boat gave the slightest roll to starboard, and I stood, knife in hand, watching her ankles pick their way down the companionway steps. Then a plastic bag appeared.

'Have you got the booty?'

'Oh!' she said, almost falling down the steps. 'What a lovely man! He pressed this bag of scallops into my hand, closed the other one around it, and said to me: "This is a gift from Islay." I told him no, I want to pay for them, we're moving onto the island and we'd like to be able to buy scallops in the future.'

'And so you can,' he said, 'but this is a gift from Islay.'

Inside the bag, cleaned and ready for the pan, were fifty scallops. Fifty. All whoppers, freshly caught from the crystal waters of the Atlantic Ocean, which drops wet kisses on the shores of that happy island.

Clam dredger

A day or two later, when Linda was at work, I took our boat on the 25-mile journey around the shores of the island to her new home at the Caol Ila distillery. We'd arranged to borrow a mooring in the bite-sized bay, which has the distillery in the foreground, and its houses ranged amphitheatre-style up the steep hill behind so that all could enjoy the view of the bay, the restless sea passing between this island, and the neighbouring Island of Jura a mile across the water.

The water in the Sound runs fast so that my boat and I were in danger of being washed past if we didn't begin motoring toward the shore before Caol Ila Bay was even in sight.

With lucky timing we broke out of the main current just as the bay appeared, only to find ourselves amongst whirlpools, dividing the main current from a counter-current in the bay. Having spun around anticlockwise, I was quite disoriented by the time I got to the mooring whose pick-up rope, in any case, had become entangled in the underwater chain. I ran forward with a mooring line and lay on deck to try to thread it through the steel eye of the buoy, and was just on the verge of success when my boat began to drift away downstream. I had the buoy in my arms, and so was reluctant to let it go now that I was so close to success, but the tide was too strong and I fell over the side. By some miracle I spun round like a cat and just caught hold of the gunwale as I fell. The boat drifted away from the buoy and I clung on – over the side, and up to my waist in water. Several attempts to get back on board failed but with one last desperate heave I got an ankle hooked over the gunwale, and from there raised myself bit by bit until I managed to roll onto the deck.

It wasn't the arrival I hoped for. But coming at the buoy again, attempt two was successful. I snugged the boat down, rowed ashore, dragged the dinghy up the slip, tied it to a stone, turned, and caught my breath to see *Caol Ila* floating quietly at her new mooring – the Caol Ila distillery to one side, and the magnificent backdrop of the Island of Jura to the other. There was a coastal path, of sorts, which led to a deer track up the hill. I climbed through silver birch and hazel to the peaty levels beyond – smoke from which give Islay whiskies their character – and within twenty minutes' walking found myself at the farmhouse we were now to call 'home'.

***

I was just brushing some red paint onto the bare concrete of the dining room floor in an attempt to make it look like terracotta when I heard three slow knocks at the back door. It made me jump because Linda was at work, the house stood alone among the silent hills, and we didn't *know* anyone on the island. My first instinct, after years of living on board – where you don't get callers knocking on your door – was to pretend not to be there.

The farmhouse we'd moved into had been built around the 1850s as a dairy. Most of the barns were derelict, with great holes in sagging roofs, and their walls were gapped with windowless openings. The farm buildings formed a square around a grassed courtyard, in one corner of which was the farmhouse, newly renovated. The knocking came again, more loudly, making the unfurnished rooms echo, as though the caller was in the house, and in every room of it at that.

Through the obscure glass of the back door I saw a figure, covered my apprehension with a smile and opened it to reveal a man of about 65 whose face was tanned-leather from a life lived outdoors.

'Och ya there!' he said, raising a hand in salutation. In the other he tapped a shepherd's crook against the ground by way of introducing himself as a farmer.

His baseball cap – which struck me as incongruous for 'round here' – had one of those long peaks which so obtruded into his view that he was forced to throw his head back and squint along his nose to see me.

'Yes!' I said, and stepped out onto the weedy gravel to prove it.

Neither of us knew what came next so we turned to admire the sunlit hills that rose and fell all around us, with their fern, heather, and clumps of flag iris growing in the boggy margins. We breathed in great sighs of the still air and took it in turns to make little noises of approval.

'Och weel, it's a grand dee...' he said at last. 'Have you recently moved in?' he asked, seeming already to know the answer.

'Yes, about a week or ten days ago.'

'Eh?'

'Ten days ago.'

'As recently as that?' he nodded, and turned back to the hill where the white dots of distant hardy sheep were grazing, dragging their wool behind them.

'And are ya enjoying yaselves?'

'Yes, we love it – it's gorgeous.'

'Eh?'

'Lovely!'

'Aye, and so it is – I used to stay here myself.'

'Did you?'

'Yes indeed!'

'What? In this house?'

'In this *very* house...' he confirmed with a chuckle.

Sailing amongst the islands over the past few years, we'd noticed that conversations in the rural communities can't be rushed; each remark is considered, mulled over, and savoured, before moving on to the next morsel.

'And how long did you live here?' I wondered.

'Eh?'

'For how long were you living in this house?'

'Twenty-five year.'

'Twenty five years!' I turned to him with genuine admiration, at which he seemed pleased – like a celebrity who has been recognised in a queue.

'And were you farming?' I asked.

'I was – I was indeed.'

'What did you farm?'

'Sheeps.'

'Sheep?'

'Yes... and some kartle too.'

He broached the reason for his visit: 'I was going to ask you – I've got a few wee sheep want shearing. Och, I'm retired now – and there's no money in it anyway – but if you don't shear them they get caked up around their tails,' he said, naming the nearest object to the one he meant. 'Then they get the fly and the margot, and if the margot get them, then they're away. Yes indeed.' He swatted an imaginary fly with an ornamental crook that wouldn't have disgraced an Anglican Bishop, and seemed more for ceremony than utility. 'They're away.'

'What – they die?' I suggested.

He turned to me in the way that a teacher turns to a pupil who has unexpectedly correctly answered a question. 'Indeed they do,' he agreed. 'They die...' He spoke the word softly, as an undertaker might, to minimise distress. 'Anyways, I woss wantin to ask you – could I mebbe borrow the lectric?'

I was about to tell him he could – after all I was keen to make a good start with everyone, especially my neighbours – but before I could get out a word in reply he spoke over me, holding the leather palm of his hand in front of my face to stop me speaking.

'Don't worry if you can't, it's nay bother at all,' he said, chuckling amiably. 'I've got a wee chenerator would do the job fine, and if he's still broken, I can tek the beasts up to the house yonder and clup them there.' He indicated his house by wafting his stick vaguely in the air behind his head toward where a newly-built bungalow stood – though it was out of view over a hill – and when he'd finished outlining his alternatives, he laughed at how easy it would all be.

I got my word in and told him that it would be 'no bother at all' to borrow the electricity, and in any case, perhaps he could help me?

'There's no water coming out of the tap this morning – do you know where the rising main is?' I asked. He looked at me blankly as I spoke, as though my words spoken with an English accent held no meaning for him at all, until I got to 'rising main'.

'Iss it ya water?' he asked.

'Yes.'

'What's the problem with it?'

'We've got no water.'

'Where?' he said, and fell back a step to express his astonishment.

'Out of the tap – there's no water coming out of the tap.'

'Och weel,' he said, coming back to me with a smile, 'you've come to the right person... ya have indeed!' He lifted his crook into the air with both hands – like a weightlifter does a bar – and dropped it onto his shoulders behind his neck as he advanced toward me.

'It's no ya rising main at all,' he said, stopping an inch from my face. 'An' I'll tell you exarkly what it is – yes indeed.' He nodded. 'I can tell you exarkly.' Dropping back and finding himself some room, he hooked the nose of his crook into the open neck of his shirt, revealing white chest-hairs, and thereby freeing his hands, which he held in the air between us like two idle puppets. He was evidently going to try to explain something quite complicated, and the puppets were standing by to interpret for me. Choosing his words carefully, he thought of a way to make it simple, like a plumber who is about to explain to a housewife that her tap's dripping because it needs a new washer – but to avoid getting technical is going to explain it without using the words 'tap', 'dripping' or 'washer'.

'See the water for the house?' he began. 'It comes from a wee loch over yon hill.' One of the puppets pointed out the hill for me. 'And it fills a wee tunk. Och, it's no really a tunk at all but just a wee box made from concrete walls to hold your water.' The puppets drew a box. 'Well, the lid to the tunk is shot and the beasts can get in. Your problem is that you'll mebbe have a wee froggy in ya pipe.'

'A frog?'

'Yes!' He beamed at me, and a puppet tapped my chest in congratulation.

'Could you show me where the tank is?'

'Eh?'

'The tank – could you show me where it is?'

'Yes indeed.' He unhooked his crook, got the balance of it in his hand, and then gave a golfer's swipe with it so that the ferule flew just above the ground. 'Indeed I can, I can show you *exarkly* where it is.' He filled the silence which followed by prodding the ferule of his crook into the gravel between us to even out some bumps. He and I stood idly watching the work being done at our feet.

'Could you show me now?'

'Eh?'

'Have you got time to show me now?'

'Yes indeed,' he said, falling back with surprise at how quickly I got on with a thing. 'Nay bother at all!'

There was a whirlwind of preparation and he began reeling off a list of the tools we'd need. Not only did I not have them, I'd never heard of them. Seeing my blank looks, the puppets sprang to my rescue and very expertly mimed what the tools did, at which point it became apparent that the tool I knew as mole grips were in fact *chores* and what I'd been calling spanners for years should rightly be called *turnersh*. I had both, but didn't know until that moment *that* I had them. Before long we were crunching our way down the gravel track in so companionable a way that it dawned on me that this would be the first of many happy hours we'd spend in each other's company. Neighbours.

Mindful of one another's safety, we stopped at the road and looked both ways. There hadn't been a car for some hours. And in any case, you always knew when one *was* coming because you could hear it droning busily over the hills and valleys for several minutes before it actually arrived. Nevertheless, we looked both ways, then at each other – for news – and then checked again. Seeing no impediment to crossing, severally and jointly accepting the risks involved, we walked to the other side and onto the heather beyond, over a hill, where we found the water tank just as he'd described – hidden by vegetation. It was lidded by two whole – and one broken – slabs of concrete through which you could just push your head. He did.

'Ahhhh!' he said, as his voice echoed around the walls of the empty chamber, sounding like a TV detective who wants to let you know that he's onto something.

Working under his direction I got the pipe joints undone whilst he pulled some steel wire out from where it was hidden by undergrowth.

'I keep this here for this *very* purpose,' he said, and inserted the wire into the hose, metre after metre, until it stopped against an obstruction. He jumped. 'THERE YA!!' he called in a told-you-so voice which could be heard on the mainland. 'There's your problem!' And with that he began stabbing the wire against the obstruction, wearing the expression of a man who couldn't be beaten. Moments later the horrifically injured body of a frog fell onto the grass between us – bloodied limbs hanging on by threads – and died. He picked it up, and held it an inch from my nose for my inspection.

'There's you!' He beamed. 'There's ya problem – a wee froggy in your waterpipe!'

I felt my stomach do a little somersault, and wondered how much of this I would tell to Linda. Then I had one of those out-of-the-body experiences: I looked down on us, my new neighbour and me, standing face to face in this anonymous green valley, far out to sea on a Hebridean island. How was it that I – an ex-inmate of bustling London – and Linda had ended up living on a remote island, in a tumbledown farmhouse, so far from modern conveniences that our drinking water came from a pond with frogs swimming in it?

Over the next few weeks I went to Devon to get our furniture out of storage, and brought my woodworking tools back to the island, together with a stack of hardwood so I could put myself to work making slightly whacky furniture. I advertised myself in the local paper – which serves the island population of 3,000 – as making handcrafted furniture that was so inexpensive *you'll wonder how I eat*, and then waited to see what would happen. Next morning a car arrived carrying a man and his wife, both in their sixties. After a long pause on the silence of our drive, the door opened and the man slowly emerged, straightened his back with a groan, took a breath of air, sighed it out, and then ambled toward me, whilst I stood at the gate, with the confident, slow, and indifferent pace of a man who had now retired and felt he had earned it. He stopped a few paces away.

'You Justin?'

We exchanged island pleasantries, beginning with observations about the weather. At last he tossed his head in the direction of his wife, who was only then emerging from the car with two sticks.

'She wants an oak coffee table – can you do one for a tenner?'

Mark Unsworth – the island's photographer, who has a smart gallery – took me in hand, exhibited my furniture and my artwork, and sold it steadily to visitors and islanders alike.

We settled in quickly. The islanders made us as welcome as dinner-guests. Open-ended offers of help of all kinds came from everywhere, and every time we met someone we knew it was 'And are y' enjoying yaselves? Och, that's goot... that's goot.'

Mother-and-son Mary and John came round in their single-seater tractor with a crate of vegetables, and fourteen pounds of grapes they'd grown, as sweet as you'll find anywhere in the Mediterranean, because they'd heard we used to make wine.

I frequently bumped into my neighbour, Archie, and thought I had surprised him one day when I went out the back to my workshop and found him hunched over a sheep that he'd tied to a gate. We townies have a joke about that sort of behaviour and I confess I did have to have a double-take when I noticed he'd got the animal's tail in his hand and was holding it off to one side. He looked up momentarily before calling his usual greeting: 'Och, ya zthere!'

As he spoke I could hear that he was gripping something with his teeth.

'There's some serious action going on here,' I quipped.

'Eh?'

'I say, that looks serious – what's up?'

'A craw-lapsh.'

'A prolapse?'

'Indeed, aye… craw-lapsh lectum.'

'Prolapsed rectum? Looks painful.'

The poor animal looked like it was carrying a mauve ring doughnut under its tail – it was puffy, swollen and had lengths of blue waxed cotton hanging down where Archie was making the untidiest job of sewing I'd ever seen in my life.

'If the flies get in there she'll be away…' he informed me as he retrieved the needle from his teeth and took another stitch.

'If the glamour ever went out of your job, would you give it up?'

'Eh?'

'The glamour…'

'Och no, it's no meant to be pretty. It's just to hold it steady, do you see?'

Our life ashore on a Hebridean island had became both an education and an adventure. Living on the boat had taught us to be careful with resources: water, electricity, food; but our thrift was as nothing compared with that of the islanders, who were only alive today because previous generations had learned to manage their scarce resources.

One morning I emerged from my workshop with a sack of sawdust, called hello to Archie – who was 'at his sheep' – emptied the sawdust against the wall, and before I could turn to go back in Archie appeared at my shoulder.

'Are you no using that?' he said, nodding once toward the sawdust.

'What for?'

'Anything...'

'No.'

'Och weel,' he said in amazement, 'if you can think of nothing better to do with it than that...'

He knelt and gathered the sawdust back into a bag using hands the size of shovels.

'That's perfectly good bedding for beasts,' he said, then raised a finger in front of my face to correct himself. 'No, it's the *best* bedding.'

Before starting work one morning I happened to pick up a forecast: the weather outside the door was sunny with whirling breezes, yet the forecast warned that by afternoon northerly winds would reach Storm Force 10. Our mooring wasn't well protected from the north so I chucked a few things into a bag and walked down the hill to take this last opportunity to sail our boat away to better shelter.

On the shore, as I strolled I stopped to poke my head into some of the crumbling remains of shanty houses built from beach stone and driftwood. They were the homes of fishermen until as late as the 1970s, and stand now as a reminder of a lost way of life. Even today, tanned cotton sails hang from their beams; hand-knotted nets with cork-floats are draped over traditional clinker boats built of larch on oak, whose wood is now soft and wormy. And scattered on the floor, lobster pots made from hazel rods lie where they fell; along the walls, shelves sag under the weight of pots of linseed oil, copper nails and cut lead. In the eaves, where the roof is still dry, coils of coconut, manila and hemp rope hang in the darkness, new and unused, awaiting a call to duty that will never come.

Clinker boats – larch on oak

Outside I heard a dolphin blowing as he surfaced and rushed out to see him. A moment later he leapt from the water again, barrel-rolling in a huge arc, leaping for joy with a pollack in his mouth. It brought me to my senses; back to the present day.

I rowed out to our boat, climbed on board, stowed the dinghy, fired up the engine and motored away from the distillery mooring. As soon as I was through the whirlpools I felt the acceleration of the fast-moving tide in the Sound, sweeping me south. Up went the mainsail – *all* of it because the wind was so light – then I stepped back into the cockpit to take the tiller as we were slightly off-course. From there I unfurled the jib, and then sat to catch my breath.

As I sank to the seat something mysterious caught my eye astern. My view in that direction was – or should have been – of a channel of water a mile wide, framed between two islands with dizzyingly high mountains of purple and green... yet a mile or so behind me was a great white wall. Every tint of colour had been blotted out by an approaching squall which reached from the surface of the sea to the sky, like an enormous stage curtain that had been drawn over everything to the north. In seven years of living on board it was the biggest squall I'd seen. I watched it flutter as it raced over the water toward me, not quite believing my own eyes. I was paralysed, I think. I stood doing nothing, yet in less than a minute I'd be in a howling gale of wind.

'*Jesus*!' I heard myself say.

There was only time to ease the sheets, allowing the jib to sag lifelessly, then I sprang up forward to the mast to slacken the halyards so that the gaff drooped and the mainsail hung in lazy creases. With that the boat drifted, powerlessly, but not for long. I watched the squall arrive. It wasn't until it was 50 feet away that the first stirrings of wind arrived – the first signs that things were about to change. When the squall hit, it came with such violence, and so suddenly, that it knocked me backwards, forcing me to claw my way back to the cockpit with both hands, to get to the tiller once more.

In that first moment the boat was thrown over like a toy until her sails touched the water, then she broached. We began to gather speed. The boat wouldn't steer back on course; her bowsprit was pointing toward the rocky shore, which I glimpsed 400 yards ahead before that too was smudged out of view by rainfall so heavy there was scarcely room for air between its drops. Each huge droplet of rain contained enough water to fill an egg cup, and they fired down onto the deck like wet bullets to shatter, filling the air with spray. When I looked down I couldn't see my feet. The surface of the sea began to smoke – it does that when violently turbulent eddies of wind pull water off the surface, and tears it, swirling, away. With visibility down to a few metres, we were consumed in white.

Still I attempted to heave us back on course, but the tiller was so resistant to my efforts that I began to think it must have become jammed. It bent like an archer's bow, but wouldn't move. At last, bringing my whole body to bear on it – bracing my legs against the seat-backs of the cockpit – I was gradually able to force the tiller up, where to my surprise it made no difference. With the wind still overpowering the sails, and the boat flat against the water, decks submerged, the rudder tended to 'lift' the hull rather than turn it.

I could smell the beach before I could see it. The air became filled with the healthy odour of fresh seaweed. And when I saw the beach just a few yards ahead, I wasn't frightened. I felt utterly serene. I explored the beach with my eyes as we approached to get a good look at the spot where our dearly beloved boat – the boat which had given us so many adventures – would end her days; here amongst the rocks and the kelp of a Hebridean island, close to the distillery after which she was named. It was fitting.

I noticed, too, that it would be easy to clamber ashore. The beach was pebbly, already close by, and the sea was calm, not yet having had a chance to build beyond a few wavelets.

The water was thick with kelp here; its fronds snaked at the surface and we combed a line through it as we raced toward the shore. Just to windward we passed a towering stack of rock, which formed the outlier on a promontory to the deserted bay into which we had arrived. Unexpectedly I felt a kick from the helm and noticed an answering movement at the bow. She began to turn. We'd found a lee from the blast, close inshore, and with that the mast sprang up to the vertical, the tiller fell light and went over easily, and our ship's head bore away. With only feet to spare, the bow swept the line of the beach until we were sailing parallel with it, passing its stones in water so shallow I felt I could stand on the bottom. We cut an arching swathe through the kelp, pointed the bow back out to sea, found the wind again, and with that now behind us, the sails inflated with a scream, the mast strained ahead, and we surged on, throwing spray at the bow as our speed built. We disappeared once more into the whiteness of the squall.

I felt the chart bump into my calves then noticed that I was knee-deep in rainwater in the cockpit – the drains having been overwhelmed by the deluge – and the chart was floating, slopping to and fro with the movement of the storm water.

There's a green buoy which marks the end of a rocky reef on Jura's south-western shore, and a headland opposite is marked by the McArthur's Head lighthouse. We had to pass through the narrow gap between them both, but didn't see either. Keeping the wind behind we crashed along at 10, sometimes more than 11 knots, yet saw nothing in the torrential rain. Throughout all this the depth sounder remained steady at 20 metres, showing that we were in the channel, in safe water.

Fifteen minutes later the squall passed overhead as suddenly as it had arrived. The rain stopped as though a shower tap had been turned off. The wind fell light as though a door had been shut to seal off the draught, and only the dripping sails told of what had just been. We drifted along in dazzling sunshine. As the visibility cleared I was surprised to see that the islands were far astern, and that we were far out to sea. Over my shoulder I could only distantly make out the Sound from where we had come. I put the helm over, pointed the bow to the mainland, and set a course for Tayvallich – one of the safest pools of water I know, where our boat would be safe for the winter.

16 OUR RELEASE FROM CAPTIVITY

LIVING ASHORE BROUGHT US BACK INTO THE 'REAL' WORLD, and introduced us to its technological wonders. At two o'clock on the afternoon of New Year's Eve, just as I had returned rosy-cheeked from a bracing winter's walk with our newly acquired dog Scooter, blowing, and ready for a grilled kidney on toast, I heard a video-call request on Skype. I was just putting the finishing touches to a cup of tea and rushed through to answer it to find that it came from my old friend Nick Beck, now living in Australia, 10 hours ahead of us. My screen filled with an image of him slumped in a chair, dribbling, and with his hair looking as though it had been glued on. His chin rested on his softly heaving chest as he slept and each inhalation was marked with a rasping snort. He looked so peaceful like that that I hesitated to wake him, and enjoyed for a moment the view his wife must have of him most mornings.

'Nick?' I called at last.

But there was no response.

'NICK?'

Nothing.

'NICK!'

Suddenly his torso jerked with surprise at hearing my voice and he grabbed the arm of the chair to save himself from falling.

'Nick?' I called again.

'Mm?' He spun uneasily round to face the door behind him, baffled. 'Yes?' he called through it, tremulously.

'Nick... behind you!'

His confusion was complete as he spun back to face the computer, only to find my face on it. 'Ah, Scroty! There you are...' he said, composing himself, and with that snatched up a goldfish bowl with a stem on it. In its tank, four pints of red liquid splashed dangerously about. 'C-h-e-e-r-s!' he said, and chinked it against the computer screen with a crack whilst observing himself on the monitor. Deciding he could do better than that, two or three fumbled attempts later he found the camera, and chinked that instead. 'C-h-e-e-r-s!' he said again.

I raised my cup of tea. As a distraction I asked him how he had celebrated New Year's Eve and during the next few minutes received a fascinating blow-by-blow account of his evening – as full a reply as anyone could wish for – though I didn't understand a word of it.

We grew into our life ashore. For six long years, *Caol Ila* suffered from neglect as we became entangled in our new life. On days when we could – on days when we *should* – have been sailing we were mowing the lawn, or painting the outside of the house, or weeding the vegetable patch, or polishing the windows.

At its worst slump, the number of days we spent on board one year fell from 365 to just 3, and we only went out then because friends of ours, Chris and Sandy – fellow immigrants who had arrived from Norfolk to be doctors on the island, and who happened to be sailors, too – encouraged us to take the boat out on sunny days when the sea screamed to be sailed over, and to catch a few mackerel.

With so little attention, the varnish peeled, fungus grew in hidden nooks and crannies, and down below our boat smelled damp, musty and unaired. The woodworm had the place to themselves, and piles of bore-dust lay at the bottom of all their favourite boards.

Then one day, after a series of events – some of which were significant, and others which didn't seem so significant at the time – we came to realise that even in our island home, which thrustingly ambitious city people would think of as a risible backwater, we were back in the rat-race, working only to pay our bills. *What is this life if, full of care, We have no time to stand and stare.* – W H Davies (1871–1940)

* * *

Linda hadn't been well, and wasn't up to a voyage, so Mr Chesworth came along instead. We left Lagavulin at six one morning, sails up – no engine – and wafted silently out of the harbour. I looked back often at our Hebridean island home, but the weather was *so* right for a voyage that nothing now would make me turn back.

An hour later the wind died. We had to get to the North Channel – that neck of water between Northern Ireland and the Mull of Kintyre – whilst the tide was tumbling south, so we turned the engine on. I'm always a bit surprised when it starts.

By mid-afternoon we were off Belfast and popped in for fuel. The wind was forecast 'light' for a few days and, who knows, we might have to motor all the way to Cornwall. At the entrance to the marina the engine died so we sailed to the fuel pontoon. It's not behaviour they encourage but the girl who served us dismissed our transgression with a hospitable flutter of her hand. She was girl-next-door-gorgeous and happy as a lark on a hot summer's day.

'I've got the best job in the world,' she told us.

She offered us a berth for the night which, after a struggle with my emotions, I turned down – fumbling with £35, and doing the paperwork would have bought us another 10 minutes in her company.

We set off again 30 minutes later, engine on, sails up, and whirred our way down the coast of Ireland. At midnight my mum sent me a text from Cuba, where she was on holiday: 'Lying by the pool. Thinking about going in for dinner. How are you getting on?'

Fine thanks, Mumps. I helmed the boat through that night, skipping bed, because I was having a lovely time myself.

We couldn't see Dublin the following day. We should have been able to if it wasn't so hazy over the land. We pressed on south. We were aiming to get through a narrow passage of water – 4 miles wide – between the rocks off south-west Wales, marked well out to sea by the Smalls Lighthouse, and an entirely imaginary obstruction on the other side. Imaginary, but dangerous enough: Traffic Separation Schemes aren't marked on the water with buoys – only on the chart. Looking at the wilderness of water around you, you wouldn't know that you were *in* one until a tanker steamed over the horizon, coming straight for you, bow-on. So we wanted to avoid that bit, nearly as much as we wanted to avoid the rocks.

It's hard to steer a boat exactly downwind, by hand, for hour after hour – a boat doesn't like having the wind from behind any more than a peacock does, and constantly tries to turn to face it. When we lost concentration we gybed and broke the backstay. But the ships we saw – perhaps bound for Liverpool – went wide and clear.

The engine failed again in the late afternoon. I didn't even bother to find out why. It didn't matter because the wind drove. That night – or that morning – we were escorted by dolphins from half past three until ten past five. The moon shone silver onto the mercury sea, and the black backs of dolphins tore holes in its surface, blew, and punctured it again as they crashed back to the deep.

At dawn we passed the lonely-looking Smalls Lighthouse. A yacht – the first we'd seen – passed behind us, heading for Milford Haven, the large harbour on the south coast of Wales, not too far from the light. Half an hour later he was gone.

During the day, which began bright and windy, we ploughed a trough ever further offshore into the Celtic Sea. By late afternoon the wind grew light, and we were drifting. I'd just announced to Mr Chesworth that I was going below to see if I could get the engine going when over his shoulder I noticed a great shape rise out of the water like a submarine missile that's run out of steam, and then crash back in. It was a whale – possibly a humpback – broaching. It did it five more times. I was more impressed than Mr Chesworth, who was telling one of his stories and resented the intrusion.

I got the engine started. It ran for an hour, then stopped. I coaxed another hour out of it, then gave up. We drifted.

That night was dark, the moon hidden behind clouds. When Mr Chesworth was in bed, a cluster of lights came over the horizon amongst which I spotted both a red and a green light. That's not good news. The red and the green lights of a ship indicate which side you're looking at – if you can see both, it's heading straight for you. I didn't worry unduly because it was still a long way away and in any case these things usually sort themselves out. Furthermore, at sea a vessel under motor has to give way to a vessel under sail.

Ten minutes later it was closer, and I could still see both its red and its green light. Having calculated that he would just squeak by to my right, I kept to my left, but we were sailing at less than a knot, so I couldn't help much. By his lights I knew he was working, and I should have looked up the particular arrangement of lights he was exhibiting to see what work he was doing, but I was tired. This was my third night without sleep. I should have called him on the radio to announce my presence, but the radio wasn't working. When he came too close I should have motored out of his way but the engine wasn't working. It's unusual for two boats to approach so close together 60 miles offshore.

Suddenly his spotlight came on, intensely bright, and began strafing the water all around me. He'd noticed something on his radar, dead ahead, and was now trying to find out what it was. It was me. A moment later he'd found me. His light was eye-wateringly bright and it hurt to look at it. There were raised voices. The light twitched to scan the water to my left, found it clear, then back to me, and kept me so brilliantly illuminated during the manoeuvre which followed that my sails seemed to glow in the darkness. There were more raised voices, then a roar of engines, and suddenly the vessel swung into the water on my left. It was a funny sort of turn: first he came on toward me, but on my port side – I thought he was coming to yell at me – then he swung away in a loop that ended in him running away, ahead and to port.

My feeble attempts at keeping out of the way had left us at a standstill; rope and sailcloth hung limp around me. Now, with the vessel clear, I bent low under the sails to see ahead, and to get myself back on course. Something caught my attention in the darkness, and at first I couldn't believe my eyes. There in front of me was the dark hulk of an unlit tanker, silently slipping across my bow, filling the horizon right to left, and towering over me. I say unlit – it had one small red light in front, but that was so far to my left that I didn't notice it at first. It curved past me, then it was gone.

In the moments that followed, all became clear, and I realised how lucky I had been. The boat I had seen with all the lights was towing this dark hulk on a line which might have been a quarter, even half a mile long. The lit boat would have passed ahead of me, leaving me to blunder into the tow line; the unmanned towed vessel would have run me down. No one would have realised anything had happened. No one at home would have known where to start looking for us.

Towing vessel, on passage, Land's End to St David's Head, 26th August 2013… thank you for maintaining a diligent watch.

I had a brainwave about how to get the engine started, and began work at 3am, upside down in the bilge. By six I'd got it going and I begged it to *keep* going until we got to the Longships Lighthouse off Land's End – if it did we would just get round with the last of the tide; if it didn't we'd be pushed back again. Four and a half hours later, with the engine still running, I found myself a bit closer to the Longships Lighthouse – and the rocks on which it sits – than I had intended. And it was just then that the engine failed. Well, I only asked it to get me *to* the lighthouse.

A wind sprang up – a bit more wind than we needed really. It filled the whole mainsail, and for the next 30 miles, with too much sail up, we galloped past Penzance, and across Mounts Bay. It was as though *Caol Ila* had just realised we were back in Cornwall and was sprinting for home. We passed five Chinese cargo ships lying to their anchors, imaginatively given names like 7, 23, 42 and 17.

I dropped Mr Chesworth at the town quay in Falmouth, under engine, thanked him for his spontaneity and for spending six days of his life on a round trip, then pushed off. A few seconds later the engine failed again, leaving me drifting amongst a dozen craft at anchor. I unfurled the jib. There was no time to hoist the mainsail again because the danger was so close at hand. Secretly I was relieved that I would be excused that effort for so short a journey. The jib pulled us clear of the docks. Across the harbour, I dropped the anchor off the smart village of Flushing then rowed over to visit John and Pam, who were waiting on board their boat a hundred metres away with a G+T to welcome me home; a G+T and a floured fillet of mackerel, pan fried, and served in a soft bread roll. Possibly one of the best meals I've ever had.

Linda joined me the next day, having driven down from Scotland, bringing with her the latest member of our crew: Scooter is a Weimaraner dog who has deep reservations about sailing in general, and sailing with *us* in particular.

Scooter

The Cornish weather outdid itself to welcome its live-aboards home. Day after day children played on sandy beaches, the gentle wind bleached our hair, upriver the trees shook lush green leaves at us like pompom dancers as we drifted between them. Folks we hadn't seen for six years came by to say hello, calling out snippets of news. Curly, who we'd last seen the morning after he lost his old and rather small GRP boat in a catastrophic fire, now hailed us from a large stylish wooden gaffer – a boat we'd much admired over the years when we had seen it tied, month after month, to a buoy.

'You've got a new boat!' we called.

'Yeah! I came into some money, and when I saw someone on board *this* boat, working, I rowed out to have a chat. He was the owner, doing her up to sell her. So we did a deal there and then.'

Then Curly amazed me by telling me that he had become an oyster fisherman. I suppose there are people we all admire for being amongst the elite in our hobbies and interests. For me, oyster fishermen – whose skills and practices have remained unchanged for several hundred years – are the elite amongst gaff-rigged sailors; they occupy a place in history, and will probably all be beatified after their deaths. Now St Curly had joined their elevated ranks.

Drinking water was running low so we nipped onto a pontoon that is used as a kind of a bus-stop for ferries, and hastily undid one of our two aluminium deck-filler caps so that we could fill our tanks with fresh water. The ferries stop running at five, after which it is permitted to berth temporarily for exactly that purpose. However, we were taking a chance by arriving mid-afternoon, whilst the ferries were still running; we spilled onto the pontoon, falling over ourselves to be quick, dragged a hose across to the tap, and turned it on full blast to get as much water as we could before the next ferry arrived. Fortunately the tap runs at a high pressure, cutting fill-times to just a few minutes, so I left Linda manning the tap and went below to remove the inspection cover from our water tank, and watch how we were getting on. With the inspection

St Curly

cover in my hand I was startled to notice that whereas I could hear a great tumbling, swirling maelstrom of water as the tank filled, the small amount of water we had left was as calm as an aquarium of tropical fish. I looked up, blinking, trying to understand the meaning of this, when suddenly it occurred to me that the filler cap I had removed was not from the water tank at all, but from the *diesel* tank, and the water I could hear gurgling down a hose somewhere on board was filling that tank.

'Off!' I yelled to Linda.

'What?'

'Off! Off!'

'What? Already?'

'Yes – turn it off! It's all going in the diesel tank!'

Back on the pontoon there was a slight pause in our lives whilst we tried to absorb the significance of what had just happened. On a footpath, on the hill above us, a small crowd had gathered to spectate, and to fix firmly in their minds what the man looked like who was capable of putting water into his fuel tank. Walking casually and on stiff legs, I struck an appearance of extreme insouciance and – what with there being no sign of the ferry – nonchalantly pulled the hose from the diesel tank inlet and stuck it into the water tank inlet, taking time to fill it to the top, before leaving under sail, not daring to start the engine.

Mentioning my stupidity to a friend the next day in the hope of hearing that – yes – that was a mistake *he* was constantly making too, or perhaps receiving some advice about how to get the water back out of the diesel tank, someone in the background – overhearing the conversation – chirped: 'Oh well, it could have been worse – you could have put diesel in your water tank!'

You know, that's what I find so hopeful for the future of the human race – we are very good at taking an optimistic view of things. I don't think it's too much to say that that's why we humans didn't die out with the dinosaurs – *nothing* can happen to us that's so bad we can't see the funny side... particularly when the disaster about which we are being so light-and-tripping has happened to someone else.

Diesel and water don't mix. I suddenly remembered that. Diesel fuel filters even have a tap on the bottom so that water that has somehow managed to get in and contaminate the fuel (usually a drip or two – I reckoned we'd got about 40 litres) can be drained off. But from that I learned that it's fuel on top, water at the bottom. We've got three diesel tanks; we had them built specially, and at the bottom of each there is a sump with a steel pipe which rises through the tank and emerges on top. Removing the water was going to be easy. We just needed one of those pumps that you whizz round and round like a barrel organ, and a drum big enough to take all the contaminated liquid. I had a plan.

Block and tackle

No one will thank me for saying this, but sailing a gaff-rigged boat, particularly if it looks like an historic one – as ours does when the varnish is falling off – emancipates you from the burden carried by sailors of shining GRP Sloops. There aren't two ways about it: if you sail a gaff rig, people expect you to behave oddly. So no one batted an eyelid early one morning when we hoisted sail in Falmouth Harbour, tacked up through the moored vessels toward the dead end of the harbour, turned to draw alongside the Town Quay – where shops were throwing open their shutters, and bargain-hunters were slamming the boots of their cars, and extending the frames of their shopping-bags-on-wheels – and threw a bucket over our stern (which we'd remembered to tie on to our boat), and, using that in lieu of brakes, allowed it to drag us to a halt alongside a ladder set in the Harbour Wall, right next to the car park and the dust of the town. We made preparations to stay for a tide, and 'take the ground' – because from there we could buy a pump, attend to our contaminated fuel tanks, dispose of the oil at the nearby collection point *and* install the new speed log which I'd brought down from Scotland but hadn't until now had a chance to fit. It was going to be a full day.

Moored next to the car park, every time we looked up three or four people were leaning over the railings, gazing down thoughtfully on our house. They all wanted to ask questions, but weren't sure if they could trust us with them. Early afternoon a retired, bearded man draped himself over the rail and sucked in the sea air in big and knowing draughts, then let it blow slowly from his lungs, smacking his lips over it, savouring it, and comparing it with similar draughts of sea air he had tasted all over the world.

'Rain's holding off...' I called up.

He tossed his head in acknowledgement of the remark. There was a long, dignified pause before he favoured me with a question: 'Ow old?'

'Me or the boat?'

He didn't answer that quip.

'Launched in 2000.'

He tossed his head again.

'We built her ourselves,' I offered.

'Boatbuilder are you?'

'No – just woke up one morning and decided that's what we were going to do.'

'GRP is she?'

'No. Wood.'

He was impressed, I could tell, because he changed his footing on the railings.

Time and tide wait for no man and when you dry your boat against a wall to work on the hull there's a surprisingly short window of opportunity to get that work done. Before you know where you are the tide has begun to creep back in, the water is already up to your ankles and the boat will soon be afloat. But when you've removed an old impeller log, and not yet fitted the new one, there remains an unplugged hole in the hull, and you are most anxious to fill it.

'After the war, when money was scarce, I bought an old landing craft,' the bearded man began – he looked wistful, and was enjoying telling me one of his memories. 'It had great holes in the garboards, and the breasthooks 'ad turned to powder. She was mahogany on oak, of course, clench-nailed, and payed with cotton an' white lead. I knew she'd want a fair bit o' work doing but I thought to meself, lovely old boat like that oughta be saved...'

For the next hour and a half I stood there listening, smiling, poised, one finger outstretched to support a mound of silicone which was slowly going hard. I didn't want to cut him short, and in any case he wasn't going to let me. I wondered if, over the years, he'd been denied a proper audience.

With the tide over my wellingtons, I waded into the water, holding another finger full of silicone, smeared it round the hole and shoved the new impeller into position. With that I slipped back on board – rudely ignoring all onlookers – to get it fastened from the inside before the tide got to it.

It was whilst I was waiting for the tide to rise, when I would be able to check my handiwork, that I noticed so much turbulence on the water a stone's throw away I half-expected a submarine to surface. The water was *boiling*. Moments later thousands of flashes twinkled in the water beneath me as a school of whitebait rocketed past, spending as much time out of the water as in it on their way toward the harbour wall. In pursuit of them were hundreds of mackerel, leaping from the water in a feeding frenzy.

Our boat was moored in an elbow formed by two parts of the harbour wall, so when the whitebait reached the wall they turned right, the mackerel still in hot pursuit. Using our hull as a sort of roundabout, both parties began circling us at high speed. Suddenly it occurred to me that there was a free meal in this, so on their next circuit I was ready with a net, plunged it into the water just ahead of them, and pulled up two pounds of whitebait.

As we floated, leak-free, late in the day, a husband and wife came by, only just keeping control of three little girls who pulled at their arms and swung on the railings like monkeys. Linda and I were on deck.

'Do you *live* on that boat?' their mother asked. She was one of those candid people who are bright, cheerful and easy to talk to because she was unafraid of making mistakes; she asked us many personal, searching and insightful questions about our travels, and about life on board.

Her husband said nothing. He only stood expressionless, listening to the conversation and all the aspects of boaty-life over which it ranged during the next twenty minutes.

At last, to our surprise, the woman said: 'My husband would *love* to do what you're doing.'

Silence fell. We naturally looked to her husband for confirmation of the remark. He stood in silence, and unless I'm mistaken his eyes were moist. He nodded, and spoke for the first time.

'You're living my dream,' he said.

PHOTO CREDITS